VOLUI
OLD TEST.

THE NEW COLLEGEVILLE BIBLE COMMENTARY

JONAH, TOBIT, JUDITH

Irene Nowell, O.S.B.

SERIES EDITOR

Daniel Durken, O.S.B.

LITURGICAL PRESS
Collegeville, Minnesota

www.litpress.org

Nihil obstat: Robert C. Harren, *Censor deputatus.*
Imprimatur: ✠ Donald J. Kettler, J.C.L., Bishop of St. Cloud, Minnesota, December 5, 2014.

Design by Ann Blattner.

Cover illustration: Detail of *The Prophetess Huldah* by Suzanne Moore. © 2010 *The Saint John's Bible,* Saint John's University, Collegeville, Minnesota. Used with permission. All rights reserved.

Photos: pages 12, 29, 88, Wikimedia Commons.

Map created by Robert Cronan of Lucidity Information Design, LLC.

1   2   3   4   5   6   7   8   9

Library of Congress Cataloging-in-Publication Data

Nowell, Irene, 1940–
    Jonah, Tobit, Judith / Irene Nowell, O.S.B.
        pages cm. — (New Collegeville Bible commentary. Old Testament ;
    VOLUME 25)
    Includes index.
    ISBN 978-0-8146-2859-1
    1. Bible. Jonah—Commentaries.   2. Bible. Apocrypha. Tobit—Commentaries.
3. Bible. Apocrypha. Judith—Commentaries.   I. Bible. Jonah. English.
New American. 2015.   II. Bible. Apocrypha. Tobit. English. New American. 2015.
III. Bible. Apocrypha. Judith. English. New American. 2015.   IV. Title.
    BS1605.3.N68   2015
    224'.92077—dc23   2014033122

CONTENTS

THE BOOK OF JUDITH

ABBREVIATIONS

Books of the Bible

Acts—Acts of the Apostles
Amos—Amos
Bar—Baruch
1 Chr—1 Chronicles
2 Chr—2 Chronicles
Col—Colossians
1 Cor—1 Corinthians
2 Cor—2 Corinthians
Dan—Daniel
Deut—Deuteronomy
Eccl (or Qoh)—Ecclesiastes
Eph—Ephesians
Esth—Esther
Exod—Exodus
Ezek—Ezekiel
Ezra—Ezra
Gal—Galatians
Gen—Genesis
Hab—Habakkuk
Hag—Haggai
Heb—Hebrews
Hos—Hosea
Isa—Isaiah
Jas—James
Jdt—Judith
Jer—Jeremiah
Job—Job
Joel—Joel
John—John
1 John—1 John
2 John—2 John
3 John—3 John
Jonah—Jonah
Josh—Joshua
Jude—Jude
Judg—Judges
1 Kgs—1 Kings

2 Kgs—2 Kings
Lam—Lamentations
Lev—Leviticus
Luke—Luke
1 Macc—1 Maccabees
2 Macc—2 Maccabees
Mal—Malachi
Mark—Mark
Matt—Matthew
Mic—Micah
Nah—Nahum
Neh—Nehemiah
Num—Numbers
Obad—Obadiah
1 Pet—1 Peter
2 Pet—2 Peter
Phil—Philippians
Phlm—Philemon
Prov—Proverbs
Ps(s)—Psalms
Rev—Revelation
Rom—Romans
Ruth—Ruth
1 Sam—1 Samuel
2 Sam—2 Samuel
Sir—Sirach
Song—Song of Songs
1 Thess—1 Thessalonians
2 Thess—2 Thessalonians
1 Tim—1 Timothy
2 Tim—2 Timothy
Titus—Titus
Tob—Tobit
Wis—Wisdom
Zech—Zechariah
Zeph—Zephaniah

Jonah

Who is Jonah?

Jonah, son of Amittai, is introduced in the first verse of this book. His identity is mysterious. He is never named as a prophet, but his mission is clearly to deliver God's message to Nineveh (1:1-2). He has a much shorter historical introduction than many other prophets (see, e.g., Isa 1:1; Jer 1:1-3; Ezek 1:1-3; Amos 1:1; Mic 1:1). He is identified only as "son of Amittai," and there is no indication of the period in which he lives.

So who is Jonah, son of Amittai? A prophet by that name appears in the time of Jeroboam II, king of Israel, who ruled for forty-one years (786–746 B.C.; 2 Kgs 14:23-29). His reign was the last period of stability and prosperity for the northern kingdom, although the narrator of 2 Kings condemns him for continuing the worship at Bethel and Dan. The prophet Jonah, named here, is credited with foretelling Jeroboam's acquisition of territory and restoring the earlier boundaries. Is the book of Jonah the story of this eighth-century prophet? The answer is not so simple. There is no historical record of Nineveh turning to worship of Yhwh, and the style of the book is not like any other prophetic book. The solution must be sought elsewhere.

Genre and date

The book of Jonah is not the report of the preaching of a prophet at a specific time. Rather it is a fictional tale. It has been called a parable or a satire or a parody, depending on how one reads it. It has qualities of each of those genres, but none seems to fit the whole work comfortably. Possibly it is woven together from previous pieces and original material. This construction also makes it virtually impossible to date. It must have been written after the period of Jeroboam II, the eighth century, and before the early second century, the time of Sirach, who mentions the Book of the Twelve of which Jonah is a part (Sir 49:10). The portrayal of Yhwh as the sole God, sovereign over all nations, supports a postexilic date, possibly around the fifth century B.C.

How does Jonah fit in the Book of the Twelve?

Recent interest in the Book of the Twelve, the collection of shorter Prophetic Books, has highlighted the position of Jonah in this collection. In the Hebrew version, the Masoretic Text, Jonah is the fourth prophet. In the Septuagint, the Greek translation, Jonah is fifth. In both arrangements Jonah is close to Nahum and precedes that prophet. Nahum is seventh in the Masoretic Text and sixth in the Septuagint. The primary message of Nahum is Judah's rejoicing over God's destruction of Nineveh. If the Book of the Twelve is considered as a whole, the message is that God had mercy on Nineveh when it repented (Jonah) but when Nineveh again turned to violence and decimated the northern kingdom of Israel in 722 B.C., God destroyed it (Nahum). The message for Judah seems to be that only through repentance will they be saved. The reader knows, however, that the warning will not be heeded. Judah will be attacked by Babylon and most of its people exiled in 587 B.C.

Who is God in this book?

The identity of God in the book of Jonah is complex. God is clearly in charge of creation, bringing a great storm on the sea, commanding a fish to swallow the reluctant prophet and then vomit him up on the shore, bringing up a plant to shade Jonah and then killing it with a worm and strong east wind. God also cares for people other than Abraham's descendants. The Ninevites are worth God's mercy, shown by the warning of a prophet and the lifting of their punishment. God also seems to overreact in threatening disaster for innocent sailors in order to corral one recalcitrant prophet.

The strongest statement about God, however, is found in chapter 4: "gracious and merciful . . . , slow to anger, abounding in kindness, repenting of punishment" (Jonah 4:2; see Joel 2:13). This version of the Old Testament creedal statement is the crux of the book: Jonah is angry because God is forgiving the Ninevites. He declares, "I knew this would happen!" What this book omits from other versions of this description of God is the added phrase, "not declaring the guilty guiltless, but bringing punishment for their parents' wickedness on children and children's children to the third and fourth generation" (Exod 34:7). The Ninevites are forgiven immediately simply because they repented. The message of this book is not punishment and retribution but rather mercy.

Jonah

1 ¹The word of the LORD came to Jonah, son of Amittai: ²Set out for the great city of Nineveh, and preach against it; for their wickedness has come before me. ³But Jonah made ready to flee to Tarshish, away from the LORD. He went down to Joppa, found a ship going to Tarshish, paid the fare, and went down in it to go with them to Tarshish, away from the LORD.

⁴The LORD, however, hurled a great wind upon the sea, and the storm was so great that the ship was about to break up. ⁵Then the sailors were afraid and each one cried to his god. To lighten the ship for themselves, they threw its cargo

JONAH'S DISOBEDIENCE AND FLIGHT

Jonah 1

The book begins with what seems to be a typical call narrative. "The word of the LORD" comes to Jonah and God gives him a commission to preach. But this is no ordinary call narrative. Ordinarily the person called objects. Moses objects five times when God calls him (Exod 3:11, 13; 4:1, 10, 13). But Jonah outdoes even Moses. He says nothing, but he attempts to flee as far as he can, "away from the LORD" (1:3). He even tells the sailors that this is his intention (1:10). He must know that this flight is futile, since he declares that the God he fears made both "the sea and the dry land" (1:9). His situation is both ludicrous and tragic.

Further exaggeration is found in the vocabulary of this chapter. Everything is oversized. God commissions Jonah to "[s]et out for the *great* city" (1:2, Hebrew *gadol*). When Jonah attempts to flee, God sends a "*great* wind" that stirs up a "*great* storm" (1:4). After Jonah explains his motive, the sailors are "seized with *great* fear" (1:10). Jonah knows that this "*great* storm" is his fault (1:12), so he urges the sailors to hurl him into the sea. Finally, after every other attempt to save themselves, the sailors follow his instructions and the sea grows calm. Then they are "[s]eized with great

▶ This symbol indicates a cross reference number in the *Catechism of the Catholic Church*. See page 103 for number citations.

into the sea. Meanwhile, Jonah had gone down into the hold of the ship, and lay there fast asleep. ⁶The captain approached him and said, "What are you doing asleep? Get up, call on your god! Perhaps this god will be mindful of us so that we will not perish."

⁷Then they said to one another, "Come, let us cast lots to discover on whose account this evil has come to us." So they cast lots, and the lot fell on Jonah. ⁸They said to him, "Tell us why this evil has come to us! What is your business? Where do you come from? What is your country, and to what people do you belong?" ⁹"I am a Hebrew," he replied; "I fear the LORD, the God of heaven, who made the sea and the dry land."

¹⁰Now the men were seized with great fear and said to him, "How could you do such a thing!"—They knew that he was fleeing from the LORD, because he had told them. ¹¹They asked, "What shall we do with you, that the sea may calm down for us?" For the sea was growing more and more stormy. ¹²Jonah responded, "Pick me up and hurl me into the sea and then the sea will calm down for you. For I know that this great storm has come upon you because of me."

¹³Still the men rowed hard to return to dry land, but they could not, for the sea grew more and more stormy. ¹⁴Then they cried to the LORD: "Please, O LORD, do not let us perish for taking this man's life; do not charge us with shedding

fear of the LORD" (1:16). The Hebrew word *gadol*, "great," appears fourteen times in this book of forty-eight verses (see also 2:1; 3:2, 3, 5; 4:1, 6, 11). Everything is supersized!

Another literary device in this chapter helps the reader understand what Jonah is doing. In order to get away from God he goes *down* to Joppa and goes *down* into the ship (1:3). Where is he when the storm comes up? He has "gone *down* into the hold of the ship" (1:5, Hebrew *yrd*). Later, in his prayer, he will tell God he "went *down* to the roots of the mountains" (2:7). Meanwhile God is trying to encourage Jonah to get up. God tells him to *get up* and go to Nineveh (1:2, *qwm*), but instead he *gets up* to flee to Tarshish (1:3). During the storm the captain scolds him for sleeping and says, "*Get up*, call on your god!" (1:6). Later God will again tell Jonah to *get up* and go to Nineveh and this second time he does *get up* and go (3:2-3).

The contrast between Jonah and the sailors is also revealing. Jonah is fleeing from God, whereas the sailors turn immediately to their gods during the storm. The sailors cast lots, a typical Jewish action, to discover the reason for the storm. Jonah knows the reason, but hasn't bothered to tell them. When Jonah tells them to fling him into the sea (another flight from God?), they make every effort to avoid harming him, although he has brought great harm upon them. When the sea stops raging, these pagan sailors sacrifice to YHWH. Although Jonah has protested that he fears

innocent blood, for you, LORD, have accomplished what you desired." ¹⁵Then they picked up Jonah and hurled him into the sea, and the sea stopped raging. ¹⁶Seized with great fear of the LORD, the men offered sacrifice to the LORD and made vows.

Jonah's Prayer

2 ¹But the LORD sent a great fish to swallow Jonah, and he remained in the belly of the fish three days and three nights. ²Jonah prayed to the LORD, his God, from the belly of the fish:

> ³Out of my distress I called to the LORD,
>   and he answered me;
> From the womb of Sheol I cried for help,
>   and you heard my voice.
> ⁴You cast me into the deep, into the heart of the sea,
>   and the flood enveloped me;
> All your breakers and your billows passed over me.

YHWH (1:9), in the end it is the sailors who are "[s]eized with great fear of the LORD" (1:16).

JONAH'S PRAYER

Jonah 2

Jonah seems to have hoped to die when the sailors tossed him into the sea. That would be the final escape from this commission of God that he fervently desires to avoid. But God does not give up so easily. God sends "a great fish to swallow" the reluctant prophet (2:1). In popular imagination this great fish is thought to be a whale. In the Hebrew text of Jonah, however, this amazing animal is designated only as a fish (Hebrew *dag*). The Septuagint describes it as a sea monster, *ketos*, a word that then appears in the Gospel of Matthew (12:40). In later Greek this word connotes a whale. Jonah is "in the belly of the fish three days and three nights." "Three days" is a common phrase for a long time and sometimes indicates the time span before God will take action (see Gen 40:13; Hos 6:2; Jdt 12:7; Esth 4:16).

Finally, in the belly of the fish, Jonah decides to pray. It would be appropriate for Jonah in this situation to pray a lament. Instead, as if anticipating God, he prays a psalm of thanksgiving. In the Psalter the psalm of thanksgiving usually follows a specific pattern (see, e.g., Pss 116; 118): The person who had been rescued from trouble turns to God and sometimes describes both the distress and the agonized lament. Then the grateful person gathers a crowd in order to tell the story of how terrible the situation was. Finally, the whole crowd goes to offer thanks to God and to celebrate the deliverance.

Jonah begins in typical fashion. He remembers his lament and the relief that God answered him (2:3). Then he describes his frightening situation and his fear that he will never again be able to praise God (2:4-7). He

11

⁵Then I said, "I am banished from
    your sight!
    How will I again look upon
        your holy temple?"
⁶The waters surged around me up
        to my neck;
    the deep enveloped me;
    seaweed wrapped around my
        head.
⁷I went down to the roots of the
        mountains;
    to the land whose bars closed
        behind me forever,
But you brought my life up from
        the pit,
    O Lord, my God.

⁸When I became faint,
    I remembered the Lord;

My prayer came to you
    in your holy temple.
⁹Those who worship worthless
        idols
    abandon their hope for mercy.
¹⁰But I, with thankful voice,
    will sacrifice to you;
What I have vowed I will pay:
    deliverance is from the Lord.

¹¹Then the Lord commanded the
fish to vomit Jonah upon dry land.

Jonah's Obedience and the Ninevites' Repentance

3 ¹The word of the Lord came to
Jonah a second time: ²Set out for the
great city of Nineveh, and announce to

has not forgotten, however, that God was the cause of this distress (compare Ps 88). But the description of all his suffering is a way to praise God for having heard him and brought him up from the pit (2:3, 7). He intends to go to God's temple (presumably in Jerusalem) and offer the sacrifice he promised when he was in distress (2:8-10).

The fish, which was masculine in 2:1 (*dag*), becomes feminine in 2:2 (*dagah*), so Jonah seems to be carried in her womb (2:1). Is his rescue a new birth? Jonah doesn't see it that way. He finds himself in the "womb of Sheol" (2:3). Sheol was understood as the place to which everyone goes at death. It is described as a place of darkness and stillness, not a place of suffering (see Job 3:17-19). Whether God is there or not is debated (compare Ps 88:10-13 with Ps 139:8). Jonah at least believes that God heard him from there and delivered him. This prophet who was always going down is now brought "up from the pit" (2:7).

The chapter ends with the announcement that God commanded the fish (again masculine) to vomit Jonah up on dry land. The next chapter will indicate that Jonah has been returned to his starting point.

JONAH'S OBEDIENCE AND THE NINEVITES' REPENTANCE

Jonah 3

Once again God summons Jonah. The similarity in wording lulls the reader into thinking that this is a simple repetition of chapter 1. But there

13

Jonah swallowed by the sea monster, mosaic in Aquleia's Basilica of Santa Maria Assunta, 3rd century

it the message that I will tell you. ³So Jonah set out for Nineveh, in accord with the word of the LORD. Now Nineveh was an awesomely great city; it took three days to walk through it. ⁴Jonah began his journey through the city, and when he had gone only a single day's walk announcing, "Forty days more and Nineveh shall be overthrown," ⁵the people of Nineveh believed God; they proclaimed a fast and all of them, great and small, put on sackcloth.

⁶When the news reached the king of Nineveh, he rose from his throne, laid aside his robe, covered himself with sackcloth, and sat in ashes. ⁷Then he had this proclaimed throughout Nineveh: "By decree of the king and his nobles, no man or beast, no cattle or sheep, shall taste anything; they shall not eat, nor shall they drink water. ⁸Man and beast alike must be covered with sackcloth and call loudly to God; they all must turn from their evil way and from the violence of their hands. ⁹Who knows? God may again repent and turn from his blazing wrath, so that we will not perish." ¹⁰When God saw by their actions how they turned from their evil way, he repented of the evil he

---

are a few differences between this call and the first. God does not tell Jonah to preach against the wickedness of Nineveh, but rather to "announce to it the message that I will tell you" (3:2). Is this a new message? Perhaps not, but it is certainly immediate. The other contrast to chapter 1 is that now Jonah gets up, not to flee, but to go to Nineveh as God commands.

Jonah's message is short and simple, consisting of only five Hebrew words. The prophet does not identify himself or name God. He does not suggest a way to avert the tragedy. The only possible course of action for the Ninevites, it seems, is to be prepared. But these foreign people understand prophetic words better than God's chosen ones. Nineveh is described as "a city great to/for God." Not only does this indicate that it is "an awesomely great city" (3:3), but also suggests that the city is important to God and perhaps ready to turn to God. This is precisely what happens. Even before the news of approaching disaster has reached the king, the common people proclaim a fast and put on sackcloth, the garment of mourning. The king himself is extraordinarily perceptive. Not only does he affirm the action of the people and even extend it to the animals, he also declares the theology underlying this action. He understands the mercy of God.

First, the people must turn away from their evil. This turning, *shub* in Hebrew, was a primary message of Jeremiah (occurring 115 times out of the 314 instances in the Prophetic Books). Second, the people must cry out to God. The wisdom of this action is demonstrated already in the exodus event. As soon as the people cry out to God (Exod 2:23-25), God hears and

had threatened to do to them; he did not carry it out.

Jonah's Anger and God's Reproof

4 ¹But this greatly displeased Jonah, and he became angry. ²He prayed to the LORD, "O LORD, is this not what I said while I was still in my own country? This is why I fled at first toward Tarshish. I knew that you are a gracious and merciful God, slow to anger, abounding in kindness, repenting of punishment. ³So now, LORD, please take my life from me; for it is better for me to die than to live." ⁴But the LORD asked, "Are you right to be angry?"

⁵Jonah then left the city for a place to the east of it, where he built himself a hut and waited under it in the shade, to see what would happen to the city. ⁶Then the LORD God provided a gourd plant. And when it grew up over Jonah's head, giving shade that relieved him of

calls Moses to lead them out of Egypt. Later, in the pioneer period, a pattern emerges: the people sin; God sends an oppressor; they cry out; God raises up a judge to deliver them (see Judg 3:7-9, 12-30, etc.). The king's final statement shows a deep understanding of God: "Who knows? God may again repent" (3:9). This insight also appears often in the prophets. Joel exhorts the people: "Perhaps [God] will again relent / and leave behind a blessing" (Joel 2:14). Two characteristics of God appear in the king's statement. God is not compelled to act if the people mend their ways. "Who knows?" God is still free. But God is very likely to relent or repent (Hebrew *niham*; see Jer 18:18; 26:3, 13, 19; 42:10; Joel 2:13-14; Amos 7:3, 6).

JONAH'S ANGER AND GOD'S REPROOF

Jonah 4

Jonah is defeated by his own success. He is also a failure: he predicted that Nineveh would be destroyed, but because of their repentance God has spared the Ninevites. The Hebrew text of 4:1 reveals a stronger emotion than the NABRE translation: this was exceedingly evil to Jonah and he was on fire with anger. Jonah again prays to the Lord (see 2:2), but this prayer is a challenge to God. He accuses God of setting him up and wants to die. This wish may have been his desire when he asked the sailors to throw him into the sea (1:12), but now it is more intense: "it is better for me to die than to live" (4:3). God echoes Jonah's words, but goes directly to the root of Jonah's desire: Is it good/better for you to be angry?

The reason for Jonah's anger is God's very nature. Jonah's faith is strong. He firmly believes the teaching of who God is: "gracious and merciful, slow to anger, abounding in kindness, repenting of punishment" (4:2).

15

any discomfort, Jonah was greatly delighted with the plant. ⁷But the next morning at dawn God provided a worm that attacked the plant, so that it withered. ⁸And when the sun arose, God provided a scorching east wind; and the sun beat upon Jonah's head till he became faint. Then he wished for death, saying, "It is better for me to die than to live."

⁹But God said to Jonah, "Do you have a right to be angry over the gourd plant?" Jonah answered, "I have a right to be angry—angry enough to die." ¹⁰Then the LORD said, "You are concerned over the gourd plant which cost

---

This description of God occurs in various forms throughout the Old Testament and is found in the Pentateuch, Historical Books, Prophets, Psalms, and Wisdom (Exod 34:6-7; Num 14:18; Neh 9:31; Joel 2:13; Pss 86:5; 103:8; 145:8; Wis 11:23; 15:1; Sir 2:11, 18). The foundational statement in Exodus declares both God's great love and mercy and also God's just punishment for sin (see also Num 14:18; Neh 9:30-31). Jonah, like Joel, emphasizes only God's merciful love (Joel 2:13; see also Pss 86:5; 103:8; 145:8; Wis 11:23; 15:1; Sir 2:11, 18).

Three of the terms used to describe God are "merciful," "kindness," and "repenting." The Hebrew word translated "mercy" (*rahum*) is derived from the word meaning "womb" (*raham*). This word connotes a mother's compassionate care for her child. The Hebrew word translated "kindness" is *hesed*, the deep, faithful, loyal love that is strong as death. The Hebrew word for "repent" or "relent," *niham*, is predicated of God much more often as it is of people. God changes the divine mind far more often than sinners do. Jonah's reason for fleeing to Tarshish showed his great awareness of God's nature. God is indeed far more likely to forgive than to punish.

Now God sets out to be merciful to Jonah and to give Jonah a God's-eye view of the situation with Nineveh (4:5-8). Jonah leaves the "city," a word repeated in 4:5 to remind the reader that the focus of this story is the wicked, repenting city. He builds a hut (Hebrew *sukkah*) and waits to see if God really is going to forgive the city. But God cares as much about Jonah as about Nineveh, so God provides (literally "appoints") a *qiqayon* plant to shade Jonah from the hot sun. (God has already appointed the great fish in ch. 2.) For the first time we hear that Jonah is delighted, rejoicing with a great joy. God is not finished with the lesson, however. God then appoints a worm to destroy the plant. Finally God also appoints a hot east wind. Jonah is furious. Again he declares that it is better to die than live.

Several terms in this paragraph are significant. Two echo the exodus event. God appoints the *qiqayon* to "deliver" Jonah just as God delivered the people from Egypt (Exod 3:8; 6:6; 12:27; Judg 6:9; 8:34). God also

you no effort and which you did not grow; it came up in one night and in one night it perished. ¹¹And should I not be concerned over the great city of Nineveh, in which there are more than a hundred and twenty thousand persons who cannot know their right hand from their left, not to mention all the animals?"

---

appointed the east wind in Exodus to make a path through the sea (Exod 14:21). God is now attempting to rescue Jonah from his own bad temper. The word *qiqayon* occurs only here in the Hebrew Bible. It is translated variously as "gourd plant," "cucumber," "bush," "ivy." Ironically it sounds in Hebrew like "vomit Jonah." The Hebrew word for "vomit" is *qiq* and *yon* suggests Jonah (Hebrew *yonah*).

Jonah is burning with anger again and God asks the same question: Is it better for you to burn? Jonah replies that it is better, enough to die. Now comes God's lesson for Jonah. Jonah pities the *qiqayon*, for which he expended no effort or care. Should God not pity Nineveh, even the animals who repented along with the people? In the same passage in which he proclaimed God gracious and merciful, the prophet Joel exhorted the people to cry out to God, "Spare your people, Lord!" (Joel 2:17). Here God pities the Ninevites. The implication is that Jonah should not only pity the *qiqayon*, but also Nineveh. The question remains unanswered and so is still addressed to the reader. Who is it that we are now called to pity and forgive?

Tobit

Who is Tobit?

Tobit is a good and holy man. He makes every effort to observe God's law and to teach his son Tobiah to do the same. His goodness is attested by Raphael, who praises his prayer and his attention to burying the dead (12:12-13), and by Raguel, who describes him as "righteous and charitable" (7:7). But Tobit has his flaws. In the early part of the story he seems preoccupied by money. He will send his only son on a dangerous journey to regain the money he deposited with Gabael (4:2; 4:20–5:3). It is Tobit's wife Anna who declares that the son's life is more important than the money (5:18-20). But money is still uppermost in Tobit's mind. Weeks later when Tobiah is delayed he worries that there was no one to give him the money (10:2). He also, however, gives alms to the poor and encourages Tobiah to do the same (4:7-11). At the end of the story he is willing to give the guide Azariah (Raphael) half the money they have brought back (12:4-5). Tobit is also greatly distressed by his need to be supported by his wife's work. He shares the sentiment of his contemporary, Ben Sira, who says, "Harsh is the slavery and great the shame / when a wife supports her husband" (Sir 25:22; cf. Tob 2:11-14).

At the end of the story it is evident that Tobit also is a person of hope. His prayer begins with a strong encouragement to trust in God even in the midst of suffering (13:1-8). Then he proclaims the glory of a future Jerusalem, rebuilt with a glorious temple as its center (13:9-18). In his final exhortation to Tobiah and his family Tobit assures them that, after the exile, Jerusalem will be rebuilt and faithful people will be gathered to it again (14:4b-7).

Theology: prayer and almsgiving

The theological stance of the book of Tobit is based on the book of Deuteronomy. Fidelity to the law and the conviction that Jerusalem is the place one must offer sacrificial worship are strong Deuteronomic themes. There is also a belief that God rewards fidelity and punishes wrongdoing. This story, however, challenges that belief somewhat. Tobit, a faithful man, is eventually rewarded, but he initially endures heartrending suffering.

Two primary virtues are emphasized in this book: prayer and almsgiving. The characters turn to prayer frequently and in all situations. There are several formal prayers. When it seems their lives are all but lost, both Tobit and Sarah pray to God (3:2-6, 11-15). "At that very time" God heard the prayer of both and sent Raphael to heal their distress (3:16), although the two characters will have to wait some time to know their prayer has been answered. Tobiah and Sarah pray for blessing and safety on their wedding night, as Raphael has instructed them to do (8:4-8). Raguel with Edna blesses God that the disaster he feared has not happened and asks for blessings for the newlyweds (8:15-17). Tobit blesses God for the gift of renewed sight (11:14-15). Finally Tobit sings a long song of thanksgiving and hopeful praise for the new Jerusalem (ch. 13).

It is not only formal prayers, however, but the spirit of prayer that permeates the book. All the characters are drawn to prayer frequently. At the very beginning Tobit testifies to his fidelity in worshiping in Jerusalem (1:6). When Tobiah and Raphael leave on their journey, Tobit blesses Raphael and, ironically, prays that God will send an angel to protect Tobiah (5:17). Both Raguel and Edna pray for safety for Tobiah and Sarah as they marry (7:12, 17). Gabael, who holds Tobit's money, also blesses Tobiah and Sarah (9:6). As Tobiah and Sarah set out to return to Nineveh, both Raguel and Edna bless the two and Tobiah blesses them in turn (10:11-13). When Sarah arrives in Nineveh, Tobit blesses her and her parents and Tobiah (11:17). Raphael instructs Tobit and Tobiah to thank God for all the blessings they have received, and informs them that he was sent in answer to their prayers (12:6, 12-14). He encourages them to "bless God every day" (12:18, 20). In the last verse of the book we read that Tobiah "blessed the Lord God forever and ever" (14:15).

The other major virtue that is stressed throughout the book is almsgiving. In the early second century B.C. this became a prominent theme in both Tobit and Sirach (see Sir 3:30; 7:10; 29:8, 12; 35:4). In Tobit's instruction to Tobiah he emphasizes the necessity of giving to the poor. This generosity is tempered by wisdom: "Give in proportion to what you own" (4:8). He returns to the theme a few verses later: "Whatever you have left over, give away as alms" (4:16). But his strongest statement is in the center of his speech: "almsgiving delivers from death" and "is a worthy offering in the sight of the Most High" (4:10, 11). Almsgiving is praised above every other virtue. It is better than wealth; it is even better than "[p]rayer with fasting." It removes sin and is the way to "a full life" (12:8-9). Tobit gave alms throughout his life, and at the end exhorted Tobiah and his children "to do what is right and to give alms" (14:9). He also used the story of Ahiqar as an example. Ahiqar escaped the plot his nephew set for him because he gave alms (14:10-11). Tobit's final exhortation is to give alms.

The book also contributes much to the developing theology of angels. Raphael identifies himself as one of the seven angels who stand in the presence of God. He is sent as a messenger, the essential meaning of the word "angel." He hides his identity in order to allow the human characters to be free throughout the story. But at the end he reveals himself and, after encouraging them to praise God, ascends to heaven.

Intertextuality

A major characteristic of this book is the allusion to earlier biblical texts. In his prayer, Tobit is so discouraged he prays to die. Here he is following the example of noble predecessors: Moses (Num 11:15) and Elijah (1 Kgs 19:4; see also Jonah 4:3). At the end of the story Tobit, like Moses, dies outside the Promised Land but looks forward to its future (see Deut 31:7-8; 32:44-52). The meeting between Tobiah and the family of Raguel (7:1-6) is patterned on the meeting between Jacob and the family of Laban in Genesis (Gen 29:4-14). In Tobiah's prayer he suggests that he and Sarah are modeled on Adam and Eve (Tob 8:6). Raphael's character echoes that of earlier biblical angels: the angel who appeared to Manoah and his wife who asks, "Why do you ask my name?" and who also ascends to heaven (Judg 13:18, 20; Tob 5:12; 12:20).

Genre and date

The book of Tobit is a biblical novella, that is, a short, fictional tale told to make a point and to encourage its readers to greater fidelity. Its purpose is not to recount history but rather both to entertain and to edify. This story is rich with irony, the situation where the reader knows more than the characters. For example, the reader knows that Raphael is an angel, but Tobit and Tobiah do not. The irony is often amusing, but this story is not a comedy. It is a serious meditation on the mystery of human suffering and God's justice.

There is a consensus that it was written in the early second century B.C. at which time the novella became a popular form (see also Judith and Esther). There is no evidence in the book of a belief in meaningful life after death, a belief that began to emerge in the mid-second century around the time of the Maccabees. It shares its theology and worldview with the book of Sirach, which was written around the same time.

Original language, place of composition, and canonical status

The original language was most likely Aramaic, although this is still a subject of debate. Fragments of the work in both Aramaic and Hebrew were found among the Dead Sea scrolls. There are two major Greek translations, one represented by Codex Vaticanus and Codex Alexandrinus and the other by Codex Sinaiticus, plus other fragmentary manuscripts. It is also included in the Vulgate even though Jerome did not want to translate it. He was only persuaded to do it by some friends who were bishops and he claims he made the translation in one day. He also made several additions, which are not found in the Semitic fragments or the Greek translation.

The question of provenance is also debated. Was this book written in Palestine or in the Diaspora? The situation of the main characters in the story, especially Tobit himself, suggests that it was written in the Diaspora. Emphasis on family and kinship, rather than city and temple, as a way of preserving identity as God's people is also a hint that the writer was not "at home." The book ends with Tobit's vision that eventually all God's people will be gathered in the new Jerusalem.

The book of Tobit was not included in the Hebrew canon, which was closed around the end of the first century A.D. One reason may be its late composition; another may be its fictional character.

TEXT AND COMMENTARY

Tobit

1 ¹This book tells the story of Tobit, son of Tobiel, son of Hananiel, son of Aduel, son of Gabael, son of Raphael, son of Raguel, of the family of Asiel and the tribe of Naphtali. ²During the days of Shalmaneser, king of the Assyrians, he was taken captive from Thisbe, which is south of Kedesh Naphtali in upper Galilee, above and to the west of Asher, north of Phogor.

I. Tobit's Ordeals

His Virtue. ³I, Tobit, have walked all the days of my life on paths of fidelity and righteousness. I performed many charitable deeds for my kindred and my people who had been taken captive with me to Nineveh, in the land of the Assyrians. ⁴When I lived as a young man in my own country, in the land of Israel, the entire tribe of my ancestor

TOBIT'S VIRTUE AND COURAGE

Tobit 1

Tobit is introduced with a seven-member genealogy, tracing him back to the tribe of Naphtali. The names of his ancestors all end in "el," meaning "God." Tobit's own name seems to be a nickname. In the Aramaic version of the story, probably the original, he is called "Tobi," perhaps short for "Tobi-el" or "Tobi-yahu," meaning "God/Yʜwʜ is my good." Tobit lived in the area settled by his tribe, that is, the northern kingdom known as Israel. The ten tribes making up this northern kingdom had separated from the southern tribe of Judah in the tenth century. Tobit's story is set toward the turn of the eighth–seventh century b.c., the time of the collapse of the northern kingdom.

The Assyrian kings had been harassing Israel for some time, demanding tribute and taking over territory. When King Jeroboam II, whose reign was one of the longest in Israel's history (786–746), died, his son Zechariah, who was pro-Assyrian, was killed within six months by the anti-Assyrian, Shallum. Shallum's reign, however, only lasted a month and he was assassinated by Menahem. Menahem paid tribute to the Assyrian leader Tiglath-Pileser III, and managed to hold the throne from 745 to 738. He was succeeded by his son, Pekahiah, who was pro-Assyrian. But

Naphtali broke away from the house of David, my ancestor, and from Jerusalem, the city that had been singled out of all Israel's tribes that all Israel might offer sacrifice there. It was the place where the temple, God's dwelling, had been built and consecrated for all generations to come. ⁵All my kindred, as well as the house of Naphtali, my ancestor, used to offer sacrifice on every hilltop in Galilee to the calf that Jeroboam, king of Israel, had made in Dan.

⁶But I alone used to go often to Jerusalem for the festivals, as was prescribed for all Israel by longstanding decree. Bringing with me the first fruits of crops, the firstlings of the flock, the tithes of livestock, and the first shearings of sheep, I used to hasten to Jerusalem ⁷and present them to the priests, Aaron's sons, at the altar. To the Levites ministering in Jerusalem I used to give the tithe of grain, wine, olive oil, pomegranates, figs, and other fruits. Six years

---

before the year was out, Pekahiah was murdered by one of his officers, Pekah, who was anti-Assyrian. Pekah attempted to organize a coalition against Assyria (see Isa 7) and was killed by Tiglath-Pileser III. The Assyrians put Hoshea on the throne, but he rebelled against Assyria when Tiglath-Pileser died. Shalmaneser V, his successor, then attacked in 724 and Israel fell to his successor Sargon II in 722.

There is a problem with the listing of kings in the book of Tobit. Shalmaneser V (727–722 B.C.) was succeeded by Sargon II (722–705), not Sennacherib (705–681), as Tobit says (1:15). Sennacherib was the son of Sargon II, but Sargon was not a son of Shalmaneser V. Sennacherib, however, was indeed murdered by his sons and was succeeded by his son Esarhaddon (681–669 B.C.; Tob 1:21).

It is possible that Tobit himself was taken captive to Nineveh during the reign of Pekah in an earlier Assyrian raid led by Tiglath-Pileser III on the northern territory of Naphtali (see 2 Kgs 15:29; Tob 1:2), although he names Shalmaneser as the king. In the midst of this turbulent time, Tobit remained completely faithful to his tradition. He reminds the reader of the separation of the twelve tribes into two political entities at the death of Solomon in 922 B.C. (Tob 1:4-5). Judah (with tiny Benjamin) pledged allegiance to Solomon's son Rehoboam, but the ten northern tribes followed another king, Jeroboam, who had been in charge of forced labor under Solomon (see 1 Kgs 12). Jeroboam, not wanting his subjects to go to Jerusalem, the capital of Judah, to worship, established two shrines: one at Bethel and the other at Dan. Tobit, however, insists he continued to go to the temple in Jerusalem to worship God (Tob 1:6-8). He is there for the three established feasts: Unleavened Bread (Passover), Weeks, and Booths, and also makes the offering of first fruits (Deut 16:16; 18:4).

in a row, I used to give a second tithe in money, which each year I would go to pay in Jerusalem. ⁸The third-year tithe I gave to orphans, widows, and converts who had joined the Israelites. Every third year I would bring them this offering, and we ate it in keeping with the decree laid down in the Mosaic law concerning it, and according to the commands of Deborah, the mother of my father Tobiel; for my father had died and left me an orphan.

⁹When I reached manhood, I married Anna, a woman of our ancestral family. By her I had a son whom I named Tobiah. ¹⁰Now, after I had been deported to the Assyrians and came as a captive to Nineveh, all my kindred

---

Tobit is particularly careful about the required tithes, perhaps even scrupulous. Besides the first fruits and firstlings for the priests (cf. Deut 12:4-7; 18:1-5), he offers the "first tithe," which is the tenth of the harvest of grains and fruits (Deut 14:22-23). He also offers a "second tithe" of money, which seems to be a misreading of the Deuteronomic regulation that allows for the offerer to bring an equivalent sum of money if it is too difficult to bring the first fruits, firstlings, and the harvested material itself (Deut 14:24-25). In addition to all these, Tobit offers a "third tithe" for the relief of orphans and widows who live in Nineveh where he resides (Deut 14:28-29; 26:12). The original meaning of these three tithes, however, is this: The required tithe was to be brought to Jerusalem either in kind (Tobit's "first tithe") or in money (Tobit's "second tithe") in years 1, 2, 4, and 5. Then in years 3 and 6 the tithe (Tobit's "third tithe") was to be kept in the offerer's home area for the relief of the poor (Deut 14:22-29; 26:12). Tobit interprets these offerings as separate and is contributing them all. This understanding of tithing reflects the practice in the second century, the time the book was written.

Tobit was also careful to marry someone of his ancestral family (endogamous marriage), a practice that is described as common among the early tribes (1:9; see 4:12-13). Perhaps the most significant quality of his righteousness, however, is his care for the weak and vulnerable, especially his practice of burying the dead. All these qualities of wise and holy living he learned from his grandmother, Deborah, who appears in only one sentence (1:8), but whose influence permeates the whole book. From her he learned to obey the law. He must also have learned from her the Deuteronomic principle that obedience brings success and disobedience brings punishment (see Deut 28). His confidence in this principle, however, is about to be tested.

In the early years of his time in Nineveh, Tobit's life was peaceful and profitable. He worked for Shalmaneser and traveled east to Media as his

and my people used to eat the food of the Gentiles, [11]but I refrained from eating that Gentile food. [12]Because I was mindful of God with all my heart, [13]the Most High granted me favor and status with Shalmaneser, so that I became purchasing agent for all his needs. [14]Until he died, I would go to Media to buy goods for him there. I also deposited pouches of silver worth ten talents in trust with my kinsman Gabael, son of Gabri, who lived at Rages, in the land of Media. [15]When Shalmaneser died and his son Sennacherib came to rule in his stead, the roads to Media became unsafe, so I could no longer go to Media.

Courage in Burying the Dead. [16]In the days of Shalmaneser I had performed many charitable deeds for my kindred, members of my people. [17]I would give my bread to the hungry and clothing to the naked. If I saw one of my people who had died and been thrown behind the wall of Nineveh, I used to bury him. [18]Sennacherib returned from Judea, having fled during the days of the judgment enacted against him by the King of Heaven because of the blasphemies he had uttered; whomever he killed I buried. For in his rage he killed many Israelites, but I used to take their bodies away by stealth and bury them. So when Sennacherib looked for them, he could not find them. [19]But a certain Ninevite went and informed the king about me, that I was burying them, and I went into hiding. When I realized that the king knew about me and that I was being hunted to be put to death, I became afraid and took flight. [20]All my property was confiscated; I was left with nothing. All that I had was taken to the king's palace, except for my wife Anna and my son Tobiah.

[21]But forty days did not pass before two of the king's sons assassinated him and fled to the mountains of Ararat. A

---

purchasing agent. On one of his trips he deposited a sum of money with a relative, Gabael, who lived in Rages. Retrieving that sum of money will become a major factor in the plot of this story. But before that becomes necessary, Tobit's situation changes for the worse. A new king, Sennacherib, returns from Judea angry because of a humiliating defeat (see 2 Kgs 19:35-36). He takes out his revenge on the Israelites who are captive in Assyria. Tobit, faithful to the Deuteronomic code of charity to the vulnerable, steals the bodies of Sennacherib's victims and buries them. When he is found out, he is forced to flee and everything he owns is confiscated. In addition, the roads to Media are no longer safe, so he cannot obtain the money he left with Gabael. All he has now is his family.

His distress is short-lived, however. Sennacherib is assassinated and succeeded by his son Esarhaddon (681–669 B.C.). The new king appoints a man named Ahiqar as his chief administrative assistant. Ahiqar intercedes for Tobit, and Tobit returns to Nineveh. Who is this Ahiqar? He was known as a wise man in Assyria, and several of his sayings were preserved in

▶ This symbol indicates a cross reference number in the *Catechism of the Catholic Church.* See page 103 for number citations.

son of his, Esarhaddon, succeeded him as king. He put Ahiqar, my kinsman Anael's son, in charge of all the credit accounts of his kingdom, and he took control over the entire administration. [22]Then Ahiqar interceded on my behalf, and I returned to Nineveh. Ahiqar had been chief cupbearer, keeper of the signet ring, treasury accountant, and credit accountant under Sennacherib, king of the Assyrians; and Esarhaddon appointed him as Second to himself.

He was, in fact, my nephew, of my father's house, and of my own family.

2 [1]Thus under King Esarhaddon I returned to my home, and my wife Anna and my son Tobiah were restored to me. Then on our festival of Pentecost, the holy feast of Weeks, a fine dinner was prepared for me, and I reclined to eat. [2]The table was set for me, and the dishes placed before me were many. So I said to my son Tobiah: "Son, go out and bring in whatever poor person you

Syriac. Then in the early twentieth century, a papyrus document was discovered in Egypt that contained in Aramaic a short biography of a certain Ahiqar and several of his proverbs. The biography sets his work in the time of Sennacherib and Esarhaddon. The writer of the book of Tobit makes him Tobit's relative and helper. So the stage is set for the main action of the story.

TOBIT'S BLINDNESS

Tobit 2

The scene moves to Tobit's home, which has now been restored to him. The family is preparing to celebrate Pentecost. This feast is sometimes called "Weeks," because it is seven weeks after Passover. "Pentecost" is the Greek term that signifies the fifty days of those seven weeks (Lev 23:15-16). Passover celebrates the barley harvest and Pentecost celebrates the wheat harvest. Deuteronomy prescribes that the offering should be "in proportion to the blessing the LORD, your God, has given you" (Deut 16:10). The instructions continue with the exhortation to celebrate with one's family, one's servants, the Levites, "as well as the resident alien, the orphan, and the widow among you" (Deut 16:11). Tobit will follow these commands as closely as he can in his exile. He cannot go to the temple, and there may be no Levites in his neighborhood. But he can certainly invite those less fortunate than he is. So he sends his son Tobiah to find a poor person among the exiled Jews and bring him to this festal meal (2:2).

But the situation soon turns for the worse. Instead of bringing a poor person to the dinner, Tobiah returns with the news that there is a dead body in the marketplace. Tobit, true to form, immediately goes out and

find among our kindred exiled here in Nineveh who may be a sincere worshiper of God to share this meal with me. Indeed, son, I shall wait for you to come back."

³Tobiah went out to look for some poor person among our kindred, but he came back and cried, "Father!" I said to him, "Here I am, son." He answered, "Father, one of our people has been murdered! He has been thrown out into the market place, and there he lies strangled." ⁴I sprang to my feet, leaving the dinner untouched, carried the dead man from the square, and put him in one of the rooms until sundown, so that I might bury him. ⁵I returned and washed and in sorrow ate my food. ⁶I

remembered the oracle pronounced by the prophet Amos against Bethel:
"I will turn your feasts into mourning,
and all your songs into dirges."
⁷Then I wept. At sunset I went out, dug a grave, and buried him.

⁸My neighbors mocked me, saying: "Does he have no fear? Once before he was hunted, to be executed for this sort of deed, and he ran away; yet here he is again burying the dead!"

Tobit's Blindness. ⁹That same night I washed and went into my courtyard, where I lay down to sleep beside the wall. Because of the heat I left my face uncovered. ¹⁰I did not know that sparrows were perched on the wall above

collects the body to bring home until sunset when he can bury him without being detected. Because he has touched a dead body, Tobit is now unclean and so performs the necessary purification ritual (see Num 19:11-13). That night, after the burial, he again purifies himself and sleeps outside in order to avoid bringing the uncleanness into the house.

Tobit's neighbors mock him, reminding him that he was already in danger of death once before for burying the victims of violence. But another affliction awaits this good man. The droppings of sparrows fall into his eyes from the roof and blind him. Doctors cannot heal him, but he is not totally without resources. His kinsman Ahiqar cares for him for two years and his wife Anna goes to work to support the family. Anna thus becomes our first example of a working mother. She must have been good at her work, because her employers also give her a bonus, a young goat, probably for the celebration of the Purim festival (see Esther). Tobit, however, is so depressed by his blindness and his dependence upon others that he strikes out at his wife, accusing her of bringing home stolen goods. Anna does not take this abuse quietly. She repeats the truth that this goat was a bonus and then she aims sharp words at the heart of Tobit's confidence: his faithfulness to the law. How can he continue to believe the Deuteronomic principle that those who are faithful will be blessed and those who disobey the law will suffer? Tobit is clearly suffering. Thus he must be unfaithful to the law.

me; their warm droppings settled in my eyes, causing white scales on them. I went to doctors for a cure, but the more they applied ointments, the more my vision was obscured by the white scales, until I was totally blind. For four years I was unable to see, and all my kindred were distressed at my condition. Ahiqar, however, took care of me for two years, until he left for Elam.

[11]At that time my wife Anna worked for hire at weaving cloth, doing the kind of work women do. [12]When she delivered the material to her employers, they would pay her a wage. On the seventh day of the month of Dystrus, she finished the woven cloth and delivered it to her employers. They paid her the full salary and also gave her a young goat for a meal. [13]On entering my house, the goat began to bleat. So I called to my wife and said: "Where did this goat come from? It was not stolen, was it? Give it back to its owners; we have no right to eat anything stolen!" [14]But she said to me, "It was given to me as a bonus over and above my wages." Yet I would not believe her and told her to give it back to its owners. I flushed with anger at her over this. So she retorted: "Where are your charitable deeds now? Where are your righteous acts? Look! All that has happened to you is well known!"

3 [1]Then sad at heart, I groaned and wept aloud. With sobs I began to pray:

Tobit's Prayer for Death

[2]"You are righteous, Lord,
 and all your deeds are just;
All your ways are mercy and
 fidelity;
 you are judge of the world.

TOBIT AND SARAH PRAY FOR DEATH; GOD'S ANSWER

Tobit 3

Anna, it seems, has done her husband a favor. Her sharp words drive Tobit to prayer. In this chapter two suffering people will pray for death. The prayers of both will be answered, but not quite as they expected. The first petitioner is Tobit. He begins his prayer with praise of God. Tobit's own righteousness has been challenged, but he acknowledges that, even though he is afflicted, God is completely righteous. Whatever God does, however mysterious it may seem, is characterized by faithful love.

Now that he acknowledged God's righteousness, Tobit prays for God's mercy. He asks God to remember him. He knows the tradition. When God "remembers," something happens. In the story of the great flood, when God remembers Noah, the rains stop and the water begins to recede (Gen 8:1). When the descendants of Jacob are enslaved in Egypt, they cry out to God and God remembers the covenant. That sets in motion the great exodus event (Exod 2:23-25). Now Tobit hopes for the same mercy. He acknowledges that he and his ancestors have sinned. He declares that God's

Tobit and Anna with the Kid Goat by Rembrandt, ca. 1626

³And now, Lord, be mindful of me
    and look with favor upon me.
Do not punish me for my sins,
    or for my inadvertent offenses,
    or for those of my ancestors.

"They sinned against you,
    ⁴and disobeyed your command-
        ments.
So you handed us over to plunder,
    captivity, and death,
    to become an object lesson, a
        byword, and a reproach
    in all the nations among whom
        you scattered us.

⁵"Yes, your many judgments are
    right
in dealing with me as my sins,
    and those of my ancestors,
        deserve.
For we have neither kept your com-
        mandments,
    nor walked in fidelity before you.

⁶"So now, deal with me as you
        please;
    command my life breath to be
        taken from me,
    that I may depart from the face
        of the earth and become
        dust.
It is better for me to die than to live,
    because I have listened to unde-
        served reproaches,
    and great is the grief within me.

---

judgment against them is fair and that they have deserved the misery of exile, but still he hopes that God will hear him. What Tobit asks, however, shows the depth of his despair. He begs God to just let him die. He has lost his will to live and cannot face another day of such suffering.

At this point a new central character is introduced, Sarah, daughter of Raguel. She too is in terrible anguish. Her father, like Tobit, is committed to the principle of endogamous marriage (marriage within the clan). But although Sarah has been married to seven appropriate husbands, all seven have died on the wedding night. As if that were not enough tragedy, she is now attacked verbally by her maid, who accuses her of killing her husbands herself. The maid, angry because apparently Sarah has abused her, wants Sarah to follow her husbands into death and prays she never has children. So Sarah too longs for death and plans to hang herself. But then she recognizes the shame this would bring upon her father, and decides rather to ask God to take her life.

Now Sarah, like Tobit, turns to God in prayer. She has been well trained; she knows how to pray. She stretches out her hands presumably toward Jerusalem and begins by blessing and praising God and makes her petition for death. Then she describes her situation. Her purity is undefiled; her love for her father is clear. But she does not know the way out of this anguish. Then, surprisingly, she surrenders to God's will. If God does not wish to take her life, she will accept it. But she still begs God to take away her suffering if she must continue to live.

"Lord, command that I be released
from such anguish;
let me go to my everlasting
abode;
Do not turn your face away
from me, Lord.
For it is better for me to die
than to endure so much misery
in life,
and to listen to such reproaches!"

II. Sarah's Plight

Sarah Falsely Accused. [7]On that very day, at Ecbatana in Media, it so happened that Raguel's daughter Sarah also had to listen to reproaches from one of her father's maids. [8]For she had been given in marriage to seven husbands, but the wicked demon Asmodeus kept killing them off before they could have intercourse with her, as is prescribed for wives. The maid said to her: "You are the one who kills your husbands! Look! You have already been given in marriage to seven husbands, but you do not bear the name of a single one of them. [9]Why do you beat us? Because your husbands are dead? Go, join them! May we never see son or daughter of yours!"

[10]That day Sarah was sad at heart. She went in tears to an upstairs room in her father's house and wanted to hang herself. But she reconsidered, saying to herself: "No! May people never reproach my father and say to him, 'You had only one beloved daughter, but she hanged herself because of her misfortune.' And thus would I bring my father laden with sorrow in his old age to Hades. It is far better for me not to hang myself, but to beg the Lord that I might die, and no longer have to listen to such reproaches in my lifetime."

[11]At that same time, with hands outstretched toward the window, she implored favor:

Sarah's Prayer for Death

"Blessed are you, merciful God!
Blessed be your holy and honorable name forever!
May all your works forever
bless you.
[12]Now to you, Lord, I have turned
my face
and have lifted up my eyes.
[13]Bid me to depart from the earth,
never again to listen to such
reproaches.

These two people of different ages in different places both turn to God in prayer when they are in trouble. They set the stage for the many prayers that characterize this book. At virtually every turn, one or more of the characters pray to God. They pray in sorrow and they pray in joy. But prayer is never far from their hearts. Their trust is not misplaced. A clue that God is at work in these lives has already been suggested by the phrase, "On that very day" (3:7). Tobit and Sarah pray to God at the same time, and "[a]t that very time" the prayer of both is heard and answered (3:16). They do not know this, however. They will have to wait to see how God will respond. But God has already set in motion the events that will bring them more joy than they could have imagined.

¹⁴"You know, Master, that I am
    clean
    of any defilement with a man.

¹⁵I have never sullied my own name
    or my father's name in the land
        of my captivity.

"I am my father's only daughter,
    and he has no other child to be
        his heir,
Nor does he have a kinsman or
    close relative
    whose wife I should wait to be-
        come.
Seven husbands of mine have al-
    ready died.
    Why then should I live any
        longer?
But if it does not please you, Lord,
    to take my life,
    look favorably upon me and
        have pity on me,
    that I may never again listen to
        such reproaches!"

An Answer to Prayer. ¹⁶At that very time, the prayer of both of them was heard in the glorious presence of God. ¹⁷So Raphael was sent to heal them both: to remove the white scales from Tobit's eyes, so that he might again see with his own eyes God's light; and to give Sarah, the daughter of Raguel, as a wife to Tobiah, the son of Tobit, and to rid her of the wicked demon Asmodeus. For it fell to Tobiah's lot to claim her before any others who might wish to marry her.

At that very moment Tobit turned from the courtyard to his house, and Raguel's daughter Sarah came down from the upstairs room.

III. Preparation for the Journey

A Father's Instruction. ¹That same day Tobit remembered the money he had deposited in trust with Gabael

---

God answers their prayer by sending the angel Raphael to heal both Sarah and Tobit. The reader does not yet know that Raphael is an angel. That news will not be revealed until chapter 5. Tobit and Tobiah will not discover Raphael's true identity until the end of the story. But the angel's name, given only to the reader and not to the characters in the story, gives away his identity and mission. Raphael means "God heals." The word "angel" means "messenger," and Raphael is God's messenger sent to heal these suffering people. The other non-human character in this story is the demon Asmodeus, who is afflicting Sarah by killing her bridegrooms. The name Asmodeus means "demon of wrath." The conflict in this story has now moved to the superhuman realm. Raphael is assigned the task of subduing the demon.

TOBIT'S INSTRUCTION TO TOBIAH

Tobit 4

"That same day," the day that Tobit and Sarah prayed and God sent Raphael to them, Tobit remembers that he has money deposited with at Rages in Media. [2]He thought to himself, "Now that I have asked for death, why should I not call my son Tobiah and let him know about this money before I die?" [3]So he called his son Tobiah; and when he came, he said to him: "Son, when I die, give me a decent burial. Honor your mother, and do not abandon her as long as she lives. Do whatever pleases her, and do not grieve her spirit in any way. [4]Remember, son, how she went through many dangers for you while you were in her womb. When she dies, bury her in the same grave with me.

[5]"Through all your days, son, keep the Lord in mind, and do not seek to sin or to transgress the commandments. Perform righteous deeds all the days of your life, and do not tread the paths of wickedness. [6]For those who act with fidelity, all who practice righteousness, will prosper in their affairs.

[7]"Give alms from your possessions. Do not turn your face away from any of the poor, so that God's face will not be turned away from you. [8]Give in proportion to what you own. If you have great wealth, give alms out of your abundance; if you have but little, do

---

Gabael in Rages. He must take care of this matter immediately, since he has asked God for death. But God will answer the prayer of the two petitioners differently than Tobit imagines. The trip is part of God's plan, but not because of the money. Tobiah's journey to Rages will be guided by Raphael, who will arrange a detour to Ecbatana, which will join the two petitioners and heal both of them. The deposited money becomes almost an afterthought.

The main characters in the story, however, do not know the details of this plan. Tobit is focused on the money, and decides to send his son to recover it. But before Tobiah makes this potentially dangerous journey, Tobit wants to be sure he has absorbed his teaching on how to live a holy life. Tobit was instructed by his grandmother Deborah; now he instructs his son. His instruction follows closely the pattern of farewell discourses found throughout biblical literature (see Gen 47:29–49:33; Josh 22–24; 1 Chr 28–29). Particular characteristics of this form that are emphasized in Tobit's speech are the mention of the speaker's death, the exhortation to keep the commandments, and the promise that God will be with Tobiah. The content of Tobit's instruction closely resembles biblical wisdom literature, especially the Wisdom of Ben Sira, a contemporary of the author of Tobit (see the introduction regarding almsgiving and Sir 3:1-16; 7:27-28 regarding the instruction of one's children).

Tobit begins with family duties, specifically care for Anna, Tobiah's mother. Even though Tobit and Anna have their disagreements, they clearly love one another. Tobit is also concerned about proper burial and wishes to be buried in the same grave with his wife. He also instructs

not be afraid to give alms even of that little. ⁹You will be storing up a goodly treasure for yourself against the day of adversity. ¹⁰For almsgiving delivers from death and keeps one from entering into Darkness. ¹¹Almsgiving is a worthy offering in the sight of the Most High for all who practice it.

¹²"Be on your guard, son, against every kind of fornication, and above all, marry a woman of your own ancestral family. Do not marry a foreign woman, one who is not of your father's tribe, because we are descendants of the prophets, who were the first to speak the truth. Noah prophesied first, then Abraham, Isaac, and Jacob, our ancestors from the beginning of time. Son, remember that all of them took wives from among their own kindred and were blessed in their children, and that their posterity would inherit the land. ¹³Therefore, son, love your kindred. Do not act arrogantly toward any of them, the sons and daughters of your people, by refusing to take a wife for yourself from among them. For in arrogance there is ruin and great instability. In idleness there is loss and dire poverty, for idleness is the mother of famine.

¹⁴"Do not keep with you overnight the wages of those who have worked for you, but pay them at once. If you serve God thus, you will receive your reward. Be on your guard, son, in everything you do; be wise in all that you say and discipline yourself in all your conduct. ¹⁵Do to no one what you

Tobiah concerning his own marriage. He should follow the custom of endogamy, and marry a woman of his own tribe. To support this instruction, he lists the example of the patriarchs and the bonds of kinship.

In the midst of this instruction Tobit exhorts Tobiah to be generous in giving alms. Tobiah should not impoverish himself, but he should share in proportion to whatever he has. Later in his speech Tobit gives specific examples of how this should be done: giving food to the hungry, clothing the naked, and paying workers promptly. The benefits of almsgiving are great, equal to the offering of sacrifice to God. Almsgiving saves one from death and the darkness of Sheol. This theme of almsgiving is a major contribution of the book of Tobit and forms a foundation for the gospel message.

Tobit wants his son to be wise, so he advises him to seek out other wise persons and listen to what they teach him. Tobiah should be wise regarding himself, cultivating discipline. He should be wise regarding other people, following the golden rule: "Do to no one what you yourself hate" (4:15). He should be wise in relationship to God, blessing God and asking God to guide his way. The commandments should be written on his heart.

One of Tobit's instructions seems odd to modern readers: "Pour out your wine and your bread on the grave of the righteous" (4:17). This may reflect a practice of sharing food at the grave of family members, or it may be another example of almsgiving, bringing food to the bereaved family.

yourself hate. Do not drink wine till you become drunk or let drunkenness accompany you on your way.

¹⁶"Give to the hungry some of your food, and to the naked some of your clothing. Whatever you have left over, give away as alms; and do not let your eye begrudge the alms that you give. ¹⁷Pour out your wine and your bread on the grave of the righteous, but do not share them with sinners.

¹⁸"Seek counsel from every wise person, and do not think lightly of any useful advice. ¹⁹At all times bless the Lord, your God, and ask him that all your paths may be straight and all your endeavors and plans may prosper. For no other nation possesses good counsel, but it is the Lord who gives all good things. Whomever the Lord chooses to raise is raised; and whomever the Lord chooses to cast down is cast down to the recesses of Hades. So now, son, keep in mind these my commandments, and never let them be erased from your heart.

²⁰"Now, I must tell you, son, that I have deposited in trust ten talents of silver with Gabael, the son of Gabri, at Rages in Media. ²¹Do not fear, son, that we have lived in poverty. You will have great wealth, if you fear God, avoid all sin, and do what is good before the Lord your God."

The Angel Raphael. ¹Then Tobiah replied to his father Tobit: "Everything that you have commanded me, father, I shall do. ²But how will I be able to get that money from him, since he does not know me, and I do not know him? What sign can I give him so that he will recognize and trust me, and give me the money? I do not even know the roads to Media, in order to go

After all these instructions about how to live a holy life, Tobit tells Tobiah about the money deposited with Gabael. But he also reminds him of the Deuteronomic principle that God rewards those who are faithful. Tobit has a very clear idea of how this Deuteronomic principle is supposed to work. He promises Tobiah that, if he obeys God's law, he will be very wealthy. Today's readers have a more nuanced understanding of the Deuteronomic principle, especially because of the belief in life after death, a belief that Tobit was not fortunate enough to share.

THE ANGEL RAPHAEL

Tobit 5

Tobiah is a good son. He will obey his father. But he does not know how to do what his father asks. He needs a guide and he needs identification so that Gabael will believe him. The identification is simple; Tobit will give him half a bond (the document on which the terms of the deposit were written), which will match the other half that Gabael holds. The guide, however, will be more than either father or son expects.

there." ³Tobit answered his son Tobiah: "He gave me his bond, and I gave him mine; I divided his into two parts, and each of us took one part; I put one part with the money. It is twenty years since I deposited that money! So, son, find yourself a trustworthy person who will make the journey with you, and we will give him wages when you return; but bring back that money from Gabael while I am still alive."

⁴Tobiah went out to look for someone who would travel with him to Media, someone who knew the way. He went out and found the angel Raphael standing before him (though he did not know that this was an angel of God). ⁵Tobiah said to him, "Where do you come from, young man?" He replied, "I am an Israelite, one of your kindred. I have come here to work." Tobiah said to him, "Do you know the way to Media?" ⁶"Yes," he replied, "I have been there many times. I know the place well and am acquainted with all the routes. I have often traveled to Media; I used to stay with our kinsman Gabael, who lives at Rages in Media. It is a good two days' journey from Ecbatana to Rages, for Rages is situated in the mountains,

When Tobiah goes out to search for his guide, he immediately encounters the angel Raphael. Here the irony begins. The human characters do not know that Raphael is an angel. They do not even know his name, because he identifies himself as Azariah, a relative of Tobit. But young Tobiah should be surprised at his opening words. Tobiah has asked only if he knows the way to Media. This Azariah claims not only to have that knowledge, but even to know Gabael who lives in Rages. He also adds a comment about Ecbatana, the home of Sarah. But neither Tobiah nor Tobit have any interest in going there. This man seems to be an amazingly perceptive guide. He also seems to be very speedy, since he claims that the journey from Ecbatana to Rages takes two days, when it took Alexander's army eleven days of forced march to cover the 180 miles. The reader knows what is happening but Tobit and Tobiah have no idea.

Tobiah is happy with this guide, so he goes in to inform his father. When Raphael enters, Tobit begins with a heartrending complaint about his blindness. Raphael, whose name means "God heals," encourages him with the words, "God's healing is near." He exhorts him to "take courage," a phrase that will appear frequently in the book (5:10). Tobit then begins his inquiry. Does this man know the way to Media? Indeed. But to what family does he belong? Tobit will not entrust his son to a stranger. After a little teasing about why Tobit wants not only a guide but a tribe, Raphael gives his name as Azariah, which means "Yʜᴡʜ is my help," son of Hananiah ("Yʜᴡʜ is merciful"), and claims to be from Tobit's own family. That is enough for Tobit, who states the terms of Raphael's employment, the

but Ecbatana is in the middle of the plain." ⁷Tobiah said to him, "Wait for me, young man, till I go in and tell my father; for I need you to make the journey with me. I will pay you your wages." ⁸He replied, "Very well, I will wait; but do not be long."

⁹Tobiah went in and informed his father Tobit: "I have found someone of our own Israelite kindred who will go with me!" Tobit said, "Call the man in, so that I may find out from what family and tribe he comes, and whether he is trustworthy enough to travel with you, son."

¹⁰Tobiah went out to summon him, saying, "Young man, my father is calling for you." When Raphael entered the house, Tobit greeted him first. He replied, "Joyful greetings to you!" Tobit answered, "What joy is left for me? Here I am, a blind man who cannot see the light of heaven, but must remain in darkness, like the dead who no longer see the light! Though alive, I am among the dead. I can hear people's voices, but I do not see them." The young man said, "Take courage! God's healing is near; so take courage!" Tobit then said: "My son Tobiah wants to go to Media. Can you go with him to show him the way? I will pay you your wages, brother." He answered: "Yes, I will go with him, and I know all the routes. I have often traveled to Media and crossed all its plains so I know well the mountains and all its roads." ¹¹Tobit asked him, "Brother, tell me, please, from what family and tribe are you?" ¹²He replied, "Why? What need do you have for a tribe? Aren't you looking for a hired man?" Tobit replied, "I only want to know, brother, whose son you truly are and what your name is."

¹³He answered, "I am Azariah, son of the great Hananiah, one of your own kindred." ¹⁴Tobit exclaimed: "Welcome! God save you, brother! Do not be provoked with me, brother, for wanting to learn the truth about your family. It turns out that you are a kinsman, from a noble and good line! I knew Hananiah and Nathan, the two sons of the great Shemeliah. They used to go to Jerusalem with me, where we would worship together. They were not led astray; your kindred are good people. You are certainly of good lineage. So welcome!"

¹⁵Then he added: "For each day I will give you a drachma as wages, as well as expenses for you and for my son. So go with my son, and ¹⁶I will even add a

standard laborer's wage, and promises a bonus. Raphael in turn promises that the two of them will go in good health and return in good health.

Tobiah collects what he needs for the journey and prepares to set out. His father blesses him and prays that a good angel will accompany him. But his mother, Anna, is terrified that now she will lose her son. She scolds Tobit for wanting more money and begs him to consider the deposited funds as Tobiah's ransom. But Tobit reassures her by repeating the words with which he blessed his son: "a good angel will go with him" (5:22). Little do Tobiah's parents know how true those words are. The good angel is already in their midst.

bonus to your wages!" The young man replied: "I will go with him. Do not fear. In good health we will leave you, and in good health we will return to you, for the way is safe." [17]Tobit said, "Blessing be upon you, brother." Then he called his son and said to him: "Son, prepare whatever you need for the journey, and set out with your kinsman. May God in heaven protect you on the way and bring you back to me safe and sound; may his angel accompany you for your safety, son."

Tobiah left to set out on his journey, and he kissed his father and mother. Tobit said to him, "Have a safe journey." [18]But his mother began to weep and she said to Tobit: "Why have you sent my child away? Is he not the staff of our hands, as he goes in and out before us? [19]Do not heap money upon money!

Rather relinquish it in exchange for our child! [20]What the Lord has given us to live on is certainly enough for us." [21]Tobit reassured her: "Do not worry! Our son will leave in good health and come back to us in good health. Your own eyes will see the day when he returns to you safe and sound. So, do not worry; do not fear for them, my sister. [22]For a good angel will go with him, his journey will be successful, and he will return in good health." [1]Then she stopped weeping.

IV. Tobiah's Journey to Media

On the Way to Rages. [2]When the young man left home, accompanied by the angel, the dog followed Tobiah out and went along with them. Both journeyed along, and when the first night came, they camped beside the Tigris River. [3]When the young man

---

THE JOURNEY AND RAPHAEL'S INSTRUCTIONS

Tobit 6

Raphael may know all the roads to Media, but he starts out in the wrong direction. The Tigris River is west of Nineveh and Rages is to the east. Nonetheless, what Raphael does know well is in accordance with his name, "God heals." Tobiah is threatened by a very large fish who threatens to swallow him, just as his family's distress threatens to engulf him. But Raphael instructs him to seize the threat itself and gut it. He is to keep the gall, heart, and liver, but throw away the rest of the entrails. Then Tobiah cooks and eats part of the fish. Symbolically he has defeated the "sea monster" and now it becomes a source of life and healing for the characters in the story.

Finally, days later, Tobiah can no longer stand the suspense and he asks Raphael why he is keeping the inner organs of the fish. He has already surmised they are medicine, but does not know how or when to use them. Raphael informs him that the fish gall is used to heal blindness, a purpose Tobiah readily understands. The practice of using fish gall to

went down to wash his feet in the Tigris River, a large fish leaped out of the water and tried to swallow his foot. He shouted in alarm. [4]But the angel said to the young man, "Grab the fish and hold on to it!" He seized the fish and hauled it up on dry land. [5]The angel then told him: "Slit the fish open and take out its gall, heart, and liver, and keep them with you; but throw away the other entrails. Its gall, heart, and liver are useful for medicine." [6]After Tobiah had slit the fish open, he put aside the gall, heart, and liver. Then he roasted and ate part of the fish; the rest he salted and kept for the journey.

Raphael's Instructions. Afterward the two of them traveled on together till they drew near to Media. [7]Then the young man asked the angel this question: "Brother Azariah, what medicine is in the fish's heart, liver, and gall?" [8]He answered: "As for the fish's heart and liver, if you burn them to make smoke in the presence of a man or a woman who is afflicted by a demon or evil spirit, any affliction will flee and never return. [9]As for the gall, if you apply it to the eyes of one who has white scales, blowing right into them, sight will be restored."

[10]When they had entered Media and were getting close to Ecbatana, [11]Raphael said to the young man, "Brother Tobiah!" He answered, "Here I am!" Raphael continued, "Tonight we must stay in the house of Raguel, who is a relative of yours. He has a beautiful daughter named Sarah, [12]but no other son or daughter apart from Sarah. Since you are Sarah's closest relative, you more than any other have the right to marry her. Moreover, her father's estate is rightfully yours to inherit. The girl is wise, courageous, and very beautiful; and her father is a good man who loves

restore the sight was well known in ancient Assyria and elsewhere. Raphael goes on to tell the boy that the heart and liver are to be used to drive demons out of an afflicted person. Tobiah must wonder why he needs that medicine.

When the travelers approach Ecbatana, Raphael tells Tobiah two things: first, they will spend the night in the house of a relative, Raguel; second, Tobiah should marry Raguel's beautiful daughter Sarah, because he is her closest relative. Raphael will arrange the details with Raguel to set up the marriage for that very evening. Tobiah is not only startled, he is terrified. Apparently news of this young relative's affliction has spread as far as Nineveh. She is possessed by a demon who kills her bridegrooms on the wedding night. One of the Qumran manuscripts (4QTob[a]) says that this demon is in love with her. Tobiah does not want to die, and he is sure his parents do not want that either.

Raphael reassures the young man and reminds him of the remedy he has in his possession, the fish organs that will repel the demon. He also exhorts Tobiah to pray with Sarah that God will protect them and bless

her dearly." [13]He continued: "You have the right to marry her. So listen to me, brother. Tonight I will speak to her father about the girl so that we may take her as your bride. When we return from Rages, we will have the wedding feast for her. I know that Raguel cannot keep her from you or promise her to another man; he would incur the death penalty as decreed in the Book of Moses. For he knows that you, more than anyone else, have the right to marry his daughter. Now listen to me, brother; we will speak about this girl tonight, so that we may arrange her engagement to you. Then when we return from Rages, we will take her and bring her back with us to your house."

[14]But Tobiah said to Raphael in reply, "Brother Azariah, I have heard that she has already been given in marriage to seven husbands, and that they have died in the bridal chamber. On the very night they approached her, they would die. I have also heard it said that it was a demon that killed them. [15]So now I too am afraid of this demon, because it is in love with her and does not harm her; but it kills any man who wishes to come close to her. I am my father's only child. If I should die, I would bring the life of my father and mother down to their grave in sorrow over me; they have no other son to bury them!"

[16]Raphael said to him: "Do you not remember your father's commands? He ordered you to marry a woman from your own ancestral family. Now listen to me, brother; do not worry about that demon. Take Sarah. I know that tonight she will be given to you as your wife! [17]When you go into the bridal chamber, take some of the fish's liver and the heart, and place them on the embers intended for incense, and an odor will be given off. [18]As soon as the demon smells the odor, it will flee and never again show itself near her. Then when you are about to have intercourse with her, both of you must first get up to pray. Beg the Lord of heaven that mercy and protection be granted you. Do not be afraid, for she was set apart for you before the world existed. You will save her, and she will go with you. And I assume that you will have children by her, and they will be like brothers for you. So do not worry."

When Tobiah heard Raphael's words that she was his kinswoman, and of the lineage of his ancestral house, he loved her deeply, and his heart was truly set on her.

---

them. Raphael knows that Sarah and Tobiah have been destined to be together since the beginning of creation. But he does not know everything. Just as Tobiah does not know Raphael's true identity, Raphael does not know if Tobiah and Sarah will have children. Only the reader knows the work that God is doing here. Twice Raphael tells Tobiah not to worry (6:16, 18), and the young man heeds the angel's advice. He immediately sets his heart on Sarah.

V. Marriage and Healing of Sarah

At the House of Raguel. ¹When they entered Ecbatana, Tobiah said, "Brother Azariah, bring me straight to the house of our kinsman Raguel." So he did, and they came to the house of Raguel, whom they found seated by his courtyard gate. They greeted him first, and he answered, "Many greetings to you, brothers! Welcome! You have come in peace! Now enter in peace!" And he brought them into his house. ²He said to his wife Edna, "How this young man resembles Tobit, the son of my uncle!" ³So Edna asked them, saying, "Where are you from, brothers?" They answered, "We are descendants of Naphtali, now captives in Nineveh." ⁴She said to them, "Do you know our kinsman Tobit?" They answered her, "Indeed, we do know him!" She asked, "Is he well?" ⁵They answered, "Yes, he is alive and well." Then Tobiah said, "He is my father!" ⁶Raguel jumped up, kissed him, and broke into tears. ⁷Then, finding words, he said, "A blessing upon you,

RAGUEL'S HOUSE: ARRIVAL AND MARRIAGE

Tobit 7

Tobiah has made up his mind that he is destined to marry Sarah and so he wishes to go straight to Raguel's house. Before he can express his intention, however, there are greetings and introductions to be made. Raguel, whose name means "friend of God," is as hospitable to strangers as Tobit is. But he is struck by the resemblance of the young man to his relative Tobit. Tobiah then reveals that he is Tobit's son. At this news, the whole family bemoans Tobit's affliction; they have clearly heard of his blindness. Hospitality then moves to the forefront as Raguel prepares a great feast. This welcome and feast are reminiscent of the welcome of three strangers by Abraham, another friend of God (Gen 18:1-8). The strangers who arrive at Abraham's tent also include angels as well as the Lord.

Tobiah, however, will not eat until he has accomplished the mission revealed to him by Raphael. He asks Raphael to ask Raguel to give Sarah to him as his wife, but Raguel overhears the young man. From this point on, Tobiah takes responsibility for his own destiny. Raguel informs him of Sarah's affliction (which he already knows) and warns him of the danger. But Tobiah will not be put off until the wedding takes place. So the arrangements are made and Sarah is given to Tobiah as his wife. The wedding ceremony is typical of the period. A fifth-century Egyptian text, the decree of Mibtahiah's third marriage, describes the wedding formula: "She is my wife and I am her husband from this day forever." Raguel states it similarly: "from now on you are her brother, and she is your sister" (7:11). The terms "brother" and "sister" are frequent references to husband and

son! You are the son of a good and noble father. What a terrible misfortune that a man so righteous and charitable has been afflicted with blindness!" He embraced his kinsman Tobiah and continued to weep. [8]His wife Edna also wept for Tobit; and their daughter Sarah also began to weep.

Marriage of Tobiah and Sarah. [9]Afterward, Raguel slaughtered a ram from the flock and gave them a warm reception. When they had washed, bathed, and reclined to eat and drink, Tobiah said to Raphael, "Brother Azariah, ask Raguel to give me my kinswoman Sarah." [10]Raguel overheard the words; so he said to the young man: "Eat and drink and be merry tonight, for no man has a greater right to marry my daughter Sarah than you, brother. Besides, not even I have the right to give her to anyone but you, because you are my closest relative. However, son, I must frankly tell you the truth. [11]I have given her in marriage to seven husbands who were kinsmen of ours, and all died on the very night they approached her. But now, son, eat and drink. The Lord will look after you both." Tobiah answered, "I will neither eat nor drink anything here until you settle what concerns me."

Raguel said to him: "I will do it. She is yours as decreed by the Book of Moses. It has been decided in heaven that she be given to you! Take your kinswoman; from now on you are her brother, and she is your sister. She is given to you today and here ever after. May the Lord of heaven prosper you both tonight, son, and grant you mercy and peace." [12]Then Raguel called his daughter Sarah, and she came to him. He took her by the hand and gave her to Tobiah with these words: "Take her according to the law. According to the decree written in the Book of Moses I give her to be your wife. Take her and bring her safely to your father. And may the God of heaven grant both of you a safe journey in peace!" [13]He then called her mother and told her to bring writing materials. He wrote out a copy of a marriage contract stating that he gave Sarah to Tobiah as his wife as

wife at this time (see Tob 5:21; 7:15; 8:4, 21; 10:6, 12; Esth 15:9[D:9]; Song 4:9-10, 12; 5:1-2). Then the marriage contract is drawn up and sealed. Only after this wedding ceremony will they begin the meal.

Raguel then asks his wife to prepare a bedroom for the newlyweds and to take Sarah there. The young woman must be terrified, knowing that seven bridegrooms have already been killed by the demon Asmodeus. Her mother too dreads this night, fearing another tragedy. But Edna is a strong mother. She weeps, but she also attempts to strengthen her daughter. She prays a blessing on her, and twice she reminds her to "take courage" (Greek *tharsei*). This word is closely connected to the healings that God has set in motion (3:16-17). Tobiah himself will encourage his father Tobit with this same word (11:11). Prayer is also never far from the hearts of each of the characters in this story.

decreed by the law of Moses. Her mother brought the material, and he drew up the contract, to which he affixed his seal.

¹⁴Afterward they began to eat and drink. ¹⁵Later Raguel called his wife Edna and said, "My sister, prepare the other bedroom and bring Sarah there." ¹⁶She went, made the bed in the room, as he had told her, and brought Sarah there. After she had cried over her, she wiped away her tears and said, ¹⁷"Take courage, my daughter! May the Lord of heaven grant you joy in place of your grief! Courage, my daughter!" Then she left.

8 **Expulsion of the Demon.** ¹When they had finished eating and drinking, they wanted to retire. So they brought the young man out and led him to the bedroom. ²Tobiah, mindful of Raphael's instructions, took the fish's liver and heart from the bag where he had them, and put them on the embers intended for incense. ³The odor of the fish repulsed the demon, and it fled to the upper regions of Egypt; Raphael went in pursuit of it and there bound it hand and foot. Then Raphael returned immediately.

⁴When Sarah's parents left the bedroom and closed the door behind them, Tobiah rose from bed and said to his wife, "My sister, come, let us pray and beg our Lord to grant us mercy and protection." ⁵She got up, and they started to pray and beg that they might be protected. He began with these words:

"Blessed are you, O God of our
    ancestors;
  blessed be your name forever
    and ever!
Let the heavens and all your
    creation bless you forever.
⁶You made Adam, and you made
    his wife Eve
  to be his helper and support;
  and from these two the human
    race has come.
You said, 'It is not good for the man
    to be alone;
  let us make him a helper like
    himself.'
⁷Now, not with lust,
  but with fidelity I take this
    kinswoman as my wife.
Send down your mercy on me and
    on her,
  and grant that we may grow old
    together.
Bless us with children."

RESOLUTION:
DEMON EXPELLED, WEDDING FEAST, MONEY RECOVERED
Tobit 8–9

The critical moment has arrived. Each of Sarah's bridegrooms has been killed by the demon Asmodeus on the wedding night. But Tobiah and Sarah have, unbeknownst to them, one of God's angels to advise them and defend them against the demon. Raphael has already instructed Tobiah to put the fish entrails on the coals left there for the incense. The aroma from the fish's liver and heart certainly is not as pleasant as incense, but it is effective. The demon is repulsed by the odor and flees all

⁸They said together, "Amen, amen!" ⁹Then they went to bed for the night.

But Raguel got up and summoned his servants. They went out with him and dug a grave, ¹⁰for he said, "Perhaps Tobiah will die; then we would be a laughingstock and an object of mockery." ¹¹When they had finished digging the grave, Raguel went back into the house and called his wife, ¹²saying, "Send one of the maids in to see whether he is alive. If he has died, let us bury him without anyone knowing about it." ¹³They sent the maid, lit a lamp, and opened the bedroom door; she went in and found them sleeping together. ¹⁴The maid came out and told them that Tobiah was alive, and that nothing was wrong. ¹⁵Then they praised the God of heaven in these words:

"Blessed are you, God, with every
    pure blessing!
Let all your chosen ones bless
    you forever!
¹⁶Blessed are you, for you have
    made me happy;
what I feared did not happen.
Rather you have dealt with us
    according to your abundant
    mercy.
¹⁷Blessed are you, for you have
    shown mercy
toward two only children.
Grant them, Master, mercy and
    protection,
and bring their lives to fulfillment
    with happiness and mercy."

¹⁸Then Raguel told his servants to fill in the grave before dawn.

Wedding Feast. ¹⁹He asked his wife to bake many loaves of bread; he himself went out to the herd and brought two steers and four rams, which he ordered to be slaughtered. So they began to prepare the feast. ²⁰He summoned Tobiah and said to him, "For fourteen days you shall not stir from here, but shall remain here eating and drinking with me; you shall bring joy to my daughter's afflicted spirit. ²¹Now take half of what I own here; go back in good health to your father. The other half will be yours when I and my wife die. Take courage, son! I am your father, and

the way to Egypt, where he is pursued and bound by Raphael. The young newlyweds are safe from the demon's anger and lust.

But they have also been advised by Raphael to pray, not surprising in this book so full of prayer. Tobiah quotes Raphael exactly as he asks Sarah to get up and pray with him: "let us pray and beg our Lord to grant us mercy and protection" (8:4; see 6:18). Tobiah composes a prayer and Sarah confirms it with her Amen. The prayer is a beautiful request for a happy and holy marriage. After blessing God, Tobiah refers to the original couple, Adam and Eve. This is one of the few places in Scripture after Genesis where the two are named and it is the only place outside of the genealogies (1 Chr 1:1; Sir 49:16; Luke 3:38; Jude 14) where there is no reference to sin (see Rom 5:14; 1 Cor 15:22, 45; 2 Cor 11:3; 1 Tim 2:13). This prayer is all about blessing, and especially the gift of a healthy and holy marriage. Tobiah ends with a prayer for God's mercy, enabling them to "grow old

Edna is your mother; we belong to you and to your sister both now and forever. So take courage, son!"

9 **The Money Recovered.** ¹Then Tobiah called Raphael and said to him: ²"Brother Azariah, take along with you from here four servants and two camels and travel to Rages. Go to Gabael's house and give him this bond. Get the money and then bring him along with you to the wedding celebration. ³For you know that my father will be counting the days. If I should delay even by a single day, I would cause him intense grief. ⁴You have witnessed the oath that Raguel has sworn; I cannot violate his oath." ⁵So Raphael, together with the four servants and two camels, traveled to Rages in Media, where they stayed at Gabael's house. Raphael gave Gabael his bond and told him about Tobit's son Tobiah, that he had married and was inviting him to the wedding celebration. Gabael got up and counted out for him the moneybags with their seals, and they packed them on the camels.

⁶The following morning they both got an early start and traveled to the wedding celebration. When they entered Raguel's house, they found Tobiah reclining at table. He jumped up and greeted Gabael, who wept and blessed him, exclaiming: "Good and noble child, son of a good and noble, righteous and charitable man, may the Lord bestow a heavenly blessing on you and

---

together." The Old Latin version adds the request to be blessed with children. In the Latin Vulgate Tobiah adds an exhortation to Sarah before the prayer that they not have intercourse for three nights (8:4, Vulg.). But this restriction does not appear in any other ancient version of the text.

Meanwhile Sarah's father Raguel has gone out to dig a grave for Tobiah. He is sure that the demon will have killed Tobiah and wants to bury him secretly so the neighbors do not mock the family. Will the neighbors not have noticed that two men came to Raguel's house and only one is left? Raguel is too distressed over his daughter's affliction to consider that complication. After he has dug the grave, Raguel asks Edna to send a maid to see if Tobiah is still alive. When the maid returns with the news that the newlyweds are sleeping peacefully, Raguel and Edna immediately begin to pray. Their prayer is a joyful song of thanksgiving to God and a petition that God will protect these two only children through long lives of happiness. Then Raguel sends the servants out to fill the unnecessary grave.

Sarah's parents do not get much sleep this night. Raguel is now ready to prepare a grand celebration. He asks Edna to do the baking and goes out himself to choose the animals to be slaughtered for the fourteen-day feast, twice as long as a normal wedding celebration. In the morning he informs Tobiah that they will spend the next two weeks rejoicing in this surprising and delightful turn of events. He claims Tobiah as his own son

on your wife, and on your wife's father and mother. Blessed be God, because I have seen the very image of my cousin Tobit!"

VI. Tobiah's Return Journey to Nineveh and the Healing of Tobit

10 **Anxiety of the Parents.** ¹Meanwhile, day by day, Tobit was keeping track of the time Tobiah would need to go and to return. When the number of days was reached and his son did not appear, ²he said, "Could it be that he has been detained there? Or perhaps Gabael has died, and there is no one to give him the money?" ³And he began to grieve. ⁴His wife Anna said, "My son has perished and is no longer among the living!" And she began to weep aloud and to wail over her son: ⁵"Alas, child, light of my eyes, that I have let you make this journey!" ⁶But Tobit kept telling her: "Be still, do not worry, my sister; he is safe! Probably they have to take care of some unexpected business there. The man who is traveling with him is trustworthy and one of our kindred. So do not grieve over him, my sister. He will be here soon." ⁷But she retorted, "You be still, and do not try to deceive me! My son has perished!" She would rush out and keep watch every day at the road her son had taken. She ate nothing. After

and Edna's and promises him half the inheritance immediately and the other half when he and Edna die. Twice he uses the phrase, "take courage," the same phrase that Edna used twice in preparing Sarah for the wedding (7:17) and that Raphael said to Tobit at their first meeting (5:10).

In the midst of all this festivity, however, there is still the matter of the money that Tobit had deposited with Gabael, the reason Tobiah thought he made the journey in the first place. Now the young man is concerned that his parents will worry about his delay. So Tobiah, who has now assumed responsibility, commissions Raphael to go to Gabael's house in Rages and collect the money. He also invites Gabael to the wedding celebration. The angel follows Tobiah's instructions and makes amazing speed in traveling to Rages, which is at least a two-day journey. Raphael tells Gabael the news and, after packing the moneybags, the two of them make haste to Ecbatana. Tobiah, ever kind and polite, leaps up to greet Gabael when he arrives and Gabael prays a blessing on the whole family (9:1-6).

PARENTS' ANXIETY; DEPARTURE FROM ECBATANA

Tobit 10

This chapter tells of the overwhelming joy of one family and the overwhelming sorrow of another. Tobiah's parents are worried sick about their son. He is late and they imagine the worst. Tobit imagines various difficulties Tobiah might have encountered, but Anna is convinced her son has

the sun had set, she would go back home to wail and cry the whole night through, getting no sleep at all.

Departure from Ecbatana. Now when the fourteen days of the wedding celebration, which Raguel had sworn to hold for his daughter, had come to an end, Tobiah went to him and said: "Send me off, now, since I know that my father and mother do not believe they will ever see me again. So I beg you, father, let me depart and go back to my own father. I have already told you how I left him." ⁸Raguel said to Tobiah: "Stay, son, stay with me. I am sending messengers to your father Tobit, and they will give him news of you." ⁹But Tobiah insisted, "No, I beg you to send me back to my father."

¹⁰Raguel then promptly handed over to Tobiah his wife Sarah, together with half of all his property: male and female slaves, oxen and sheep, donkeys and camels, clothing, money, and household goods. ¹¹He saw them safely off. Embracing Tobiah, he said to him: "Farewell, son. Have a safe journey. May the Lord of heaven grant prosperity to you and to your wife Sarah. And may I see children of yours before I die!" ¹²Then he said to his daughter Sarah, "My daughter, honor your father-in-law and your mother-in-law, because from now on they are as much your parents as the ones who brought you into the world. Go in peace, daughter; let me hear a good report about you as long as I live." Finally he said goodbye to them and let them go.

Edna also said to Tobiah: "My child and beloved kinsman, may the Lord bring you back safely, and may I live long enough to see children of you and of my daughter Sarah before I die. Before the Lord, I entrust my daughter to your care. Never cause her grief all the days of your life. Go in peace, son. From now on I am your mother, and Sarah is your sister. Together may we all prosper throughout the days of our

died. Tobit attempts to encourage her by reminding her of the trustworthy guide that accompanies their son. The reader knows that he is quite right, but Anna will hear none of it. Their conversation echoes the sharp tone of chapter 2. He tells her to be still; she replies, "You be still!" Paradoxically, however, as she continues to declare that Tobiah is dead, she goes out every day to watch for his return. She is eating nothing and crying all night. Tobit too must be getting little food and sleep.

The situation at Raguel's house stands in direct contrast to the grief at Tobit's house. The wedding celebration has ended, but Raguel wants Tobiah and Sarah to stay in Ecbatana with him and Edna. He promises to send messengers to inform Tobiah's parents of the wedding and the whereabouts of their son. But Tobiah is a wise son; he knows his parents and knows how worried they must be. So preparations are made for the departure. The farewells are tender. Both Raguel and Edna pray blessings upon the newlyweds. They remind Sarah that Tobit and Anna are now also her

lives." She kissed them both and saw them safely off.

¹³Tobiah left Raguel, full of happiness and joy, and he blessed the Lord of heaven and earth, the King of all, for making his journey so successful. Finally he blessed Raguel and his wife Edna, and added, "I have been commanded by the Lord to honor you all the days of your life!"

11 **Homeward Journey.** ¹As they drew near to Kaserin, which is opposite Nineveh, ²Raphael said: "You know how we left your father. ³Let us hurry on ahead of your wife to prepare the house while they are still on the way." ⁴So both went on ahead together, and Raphael said to him, "Take the gall in your hand!" And the dog ran along behind them.

⁵Meanwhile, Anna sat watching the road by which her son was to come. ⁶When she saw him coming, she called to his father, "Look, your son is coming, and the man who traveled with him!"

⁷Raphael said to Tobiah before he came near to his father: "I know that his eyes will be opened. ⁸Apply the fish gall to his eyes, and the medicine will make the white scales shrink and peel off from his eyes; then your father will have sight again and will see the light of day."

Sight Restored. ⁹Then Anna ran up to her son, embraced him, and said to him, "Now that I have seen you again, son, I am ready to die!" And she sobbed aloud. ¹⁰Tobit got up and stumbled out through the courtyard gate to meet his son. Tobiah went up to him ¹¹with the fish gall in his hand and blew into his

parents, just as Tobiah is now their son. Raguel encourages Sarah to be good and Edna instructs Tobiah never to bring grief upon his wife. Tobiah in turn blesses his father-in-law and mother-in-law. After lengthy good-byes, he thanks God for all these gifts and sets off "full of happiness."

HOMEWARD JOURNEY AND HEALING

Tobit 11

The return journey to Nineveh is told with dispatch. What is most important now is the second healing promised by God. Sarah is free of Asmodeus and married to Tobiah; now Raphael and Tobiah are focused on the removal of Tobit's blindness. Even the dog, whose last appearance was in chapter 6 as the travelers set out, now is hurrying to get home (6:2; 11:4).

Anna, who has been watching the road every day, finally spots Tobiah in the distance. She, who has been calling Tobiah *"my* son" since he left, now says to Tobit, "Look, *your* son is coming" (11:6). She runs up to him, hugs him, and declares that now she can die! Everything she had hoped for is fulfilled. Anna never fails to express her strong emotions. Meanwhile, Tobit, having heard Anna's declaration, stumbles out of the gate. The stage is set for the second healing. A painting by the nineteenth-

eyes. Holding him firmly, he said, "Courage, father." Then he applied the medicine to his eyes, and it made them sting. [12, 13]Tobiah used both hands to peel the white scales from the corners of his eyes. Tobit saw his son and threw his arms around him. [14]Weeping, he exclaimed, "I can see you, son, the light of my eyes!" Then he prayed,

"Blessed be God,
blessed be his great name,
and blessed be all his holy
angels.
May his great name be with us,
and blessed be all the angels
throughout all the ages.
[15]God it was who afflicted me,
and God who has had mercy on
me.
Now I see my son Tobiah!"

Then Tobit went back in, rejoicing and praising God with full voice. Tobiah related to his father how his journey had been a success; that he had brought back the money; and that he had married Raguel's daughter Sarah, who was about to arrive, for she was near the gate of Nineveh.

[16]Rejoicing and blessing God, Tobit went out to the gate of Nineveh to meet his daughter-in-law. When the people of Nineveh saw him coming, walking along briskly, with no one leading him by the hand, they were amazed. [17]Before them all Tobit proclaimed how God had shown mercy to him and opened his eyes. When Tobit came up to Sarah, the wife of his son Tobiah, he blessed her and said: "Welcome, my daughter! Blessed be your God for bringing you to us, daughter! Blessed are your father and your mother. Blessed be my son Tobiah, and blessed be you, daughter! Welcome to your home with blessing and joy. Come in, daughter!" That day there was joy for all the Jews who lived in Nineveh. [18]Ahiqar and his nephew Nadin were

---

century artist Jean-François Millet titled *Waiting* portrays this scene poignantly. An old woman has started down the road and a blind old man stands hesitantly in the doorway.

Raphael has already instructed Tobiah about the use of the gall and the method he is to use to heal his father. But it is Tobiah who performs the action that restores Tobit's sight. Tobit is also overcome with joy and is delighted that his first vision is that of his dearly beloved son. Immediately Tobit expresses his gratitude to God, blessing God and all God's angels. He does not yet know that God has sent an angel to bring about his healing and that this angel is standing right in front of him.

Tobiah tells his father the whole story of all that has happened in Ecbatana. Tobit rushes out to meet his new daughter-in-law. His brisk stride amazes his neighbors and a crowd gathers to rejoice with him. Tobit greets Sarah with many blessings and claims her as his daughter. Then all the Jews of Nineveh join in the celebration of God's goodness in healing Tobit and Sarah. Another seven-day wedding feast follows; the newlyweds have now celebrated for twenty-one days! Ahiqar, Tobit's relative

also on hand to rejoice with Tobit. Tobiah's wedding feast was celebrated with joy for seven days, and many gifts were given to him.

VII. Raphael Reveals His Identity

Raphael's Wages. ¹When the wedding celebration came to an end, Tobit called his son Tobiah and said to him, "Son, see to it that you pay his wages to the man who made the journey with you and give him a bonus too." ²Tobiah said: "Father, how much shall I pay him? It would not hurt to give him half the wealth he brought back with me. ³He led me back safe and sound, healed my wife, brought the money back with me, and healed you. How much should I pay him?" ⁴Tobit answered, "It is only fair, son, that he should receive half of all that he brought back." ⁵So Tobiah called Raphael and said, "Take as your wages half of all that you have brought back, and farewell!"

Exhortation. ⁶Raphael called the two of them aside privately and said to them: "Bless God and give him thanks before all the living for the good things he has done for you, by blessing and extolling his name in song. Proclaim before all with due honor the deeds of

who helped him before his blindness, is among the guests along with his nephew, Nadin. A treacherous story about Nadin will soon be revealed.

RAPHAEL'S IDENTITY

Tobit 12

Tobit is now ready to wrap up the details of the journey. He has been healed of his blindness. His wife is happy again. His son has come home with a new wife. All that remains is to pay their debt to the guide who not only led Tobiah safely on the journey, but who brought him to his new wife and taught him how to heal her and his father. The money, the original purpose of the journey, has also been recovered from Gabael. How can they possibly reward this extraordinary guide? In the original agreement (Tob 5:15-16) they promised him a drachma per day, the normal daily wage, and a possible bonus. Now they decide to offer him half the ten talents that have been brought back (see 1:14). So Raphael's payment would be raised from about $1.20 per week, so presumably no more than $10 total, to almost $7,000 for the journey.

But Raphael has a surprise of his own. When they offer him this generous sum, he changes the subject. First, he gives them an instruction, which echoes Tobit's instruction to Tobiah before the journey. They are to continue to give thanks to God with all their energy and devotion. They are to proclaim their thanks before all the living. In the biblical tradition thanksgiving requires a crowd or at least another person. The Hebrew word for

God, and do not be slack in thanking him. ⁷A king's secret should be kept secret, but one must declare the works of God and give thanks with due honor. Do good, and evil will not overtake you. ⁸Prayer with fasting is good. Almsgiving with righteousness is better than wealth with wickedness. It is better to give alms than to store up gold, ⁹for almsgiving saves from death, and purges all sin. Those who give alms will enjoy a full life, ¹⁰but those who commit sin and do evil are their own worst enemies.

Raphael's Identity. ¹¹"I shall now tell you the whole truth and conceal nothing at all from you. I have already said to you, 'A king's secret should be kept secret, but one must declare the works of God with due honor.' ¹²Now when you, Tobit, and Sarah prayed, it was I who presented the record of your prayer before the Glory of the Lord; and likewise whenever you used to bury the dead. ¹³When you did not hesitate to get up and leave your dinner in order to go and bury that dead man, ¹⁴I was sent to put you to the test. At the same time, however, God sent me to heal you and your daughter-in-law Sarah. ¹⁵I am Raphael, one of the seven angels who stand and serve before the Glory of the Lord."

"thank" (*todah*) also means "praise." Thanksgiving is proclaiming to someone else how good God is. This move to gratitude is something they have been doing throughout the book and they are not to forget it now that their troubles are diminished. But even this public prayer and thanksgiving are not enough. They are also to continue to give alms to the poor and needy. This emphasis on almsgiving is characteristic not only of this book, but of second-century Jewish piety. Ben Sira emphasizes the same action, and also says that almsgiving is more valuable than gold and will "save [them] from every evil" (Sir 29:8-13; see Tob 4:7-11, 16-17; 14:2, 9-11).

The second part of Raphael's speech reveals a big surprise. He is not Azariah, one of Tobit's kinsmen (see Tob 5:13); he is Raphael, one of the seven angels who stand before God. His true name corresponds to his task; Raphael means "God heals." He was sent by God right after Tobit and Sarah prayed for relief from their anguish (3:16-17). He is, in fact, the one who presented their prayer to God as well as Tobit's charitable deeds. But he was sent to them, not only to heal, but also to put them to the test to determine their perseverance and to strengthen their faith.

Raphael claims to be one of the seven angels standing before God. Traditionally these angels are called "archangels." Three of them are named in Scripture: Michael, who is the protector of the people (Dan 12:1; Rev 12:7-9); Gabriel, who announces the births of John the Baptist and Jesus (Luke 1:19, 26; cf. Dan 8:16; 9:21); and Raphael, who appears only here. Tradition has given us the names of four more: Uriel (or Phanuel), Raguel,

¹⁶Greatly shaken, the two of them fell prostrate in fear. ¹⁷But Raphael said to them: "Do not fear; peace be with you! Bless God now and forever. ¹⁸As for me, when I was with you, I was not acting out of any favor on my part, but by God's will. So bless God every day; give praise with song. ¹⁹Even though you saw me eat and drink, I did not eat or drink anything; what you were seeing was a vision. ²⁰So now bless the Lord on earth and give thanks to God. Look, I am ascending to the one who sent me. Write down all that has happened to you." And he ascended. ²¹They stood up but were no longer able to see him. ²²They kept blessing God and singing his praises, and they continued to give thanks for these marvelous works that God had done, because an angel of God appeared to them.

VIII. Tobit's Song of Praise

13 ¹ Then Tobit spoke and composed a song of joyful praise; he said:
Blessed be God who lives forever,
    because his kingship lasts for all ages.
²For he afflicts and shows mercy,
    casts down to the depths of Hades,
    brings up from the great abyss.
What is there that can snatch from his hand?

³Give thanks to him, you Israelites,
    in the presence of the nations,
    for though he has scattered you among them,
⁴even there recount his greatness.
Exalt him before every living being,
    because he is your Lord, and he is your God,
    our Father and God forever and ever!

Sariel, and Remuel. In the book of Revelation there are seven angels who stand before God and blow the seven trumpets (Rev 8:2-6).

Tobit and Tobiah are terrified, but Raphael encourages them with a typical angelic phrase, "Do not fear." He exhorts them again to give praise and thanks to God. Then he ascends to heaven and they can no longer see him. The scene foreshadows Jesus' ascension into heaven (Acts 1:9).

TOBIT'S SONG OF PRAISE

Tobit 13

Tobit's thanksgiving becomes an extended song of praise. The first eight verses are praise of God who both "afflicts and shows mercy" (13:2). Tobit has come to a new understanding of the Deuteronomic principle regarding prosperity and suffering. After stating this renewed principle, Tobit encourages his people, the Israelites, to thank God who, because of their sins, has afflicted them through exile but who will also have mercy on them when they turn back to God (13:3-6ab). Then he uses himself as an example, giving thanks even in captivity and rejoicing in God, "King of the ages" and "King of heaven" (13:6c-8a).

⁵He will afflict you for your iniqui-
    ties,
    but will have mercy on all of
      you.
He will gather you from all the
    nations
    among whom you have been
      scattered.

⁶When you turn back to him with
    all your heart,
    and with all your soul do what
      is right before him,
Then he will turn to you,
    and will hide his face from you
      no longer.

Now consider what he has done for
    you,
    and give thanks with full voice.
Bless the Lord of righteousness,
    and exalt the King of the ages.

In the land of my captivity I give
    thanks,
    and declare his power and
      majesty to a sinful nation.
According to your heart do what is
    right before him:
    perhaps there will be pardon for
      you.

⁷As for me, I exalt my God,
    my soul exalts the King of
      heaven,
    and rejoices all the days of my
      life.

Let all sing praise to his greatness,
    ⁸let all speak and give thanks in
      Jerusalem.

⁹Jerusalem, holy city,
    he will afflict you for the works
      of your hands,
    but will again pity the children
      of the righteous.
¹⁰Give thanks to the Lord with
    righteousness,
    and bless the King of the ages,
    so that your tabernacle may be
      rebuilt in you with joy.
May he gladden within you all who
    are captives;
    may he cherish within you all
      who are distressed
    for all generations to come.

¹¹A bright light will shine to the
    limits of the earth.
    Many nations will come to you
      from afar,
And inhabitants of all the ends of
    the earth
    to your holy name,
Bearing in their hands gifts for the
    King of heaven.
Generation after generation will
    offer joyful worship in you;
    your name will be great forever
      and ever.

¹²Cursed be all who despise you
    and revile you;

Verses 9-18 are an exultant praise addressed to Jerusalem, the holy city that has also been afflicted but will again enjoy God's mercy. Tobit hopes the temple will be rebuilt and that peoples from the ends of the earth will again come to worship God (13:9-11). He proclaims a curse against all who hate and attack the holy city (13:12). Then, he balances the curses with a series of beatitudes, proclaiming the happiness of those who love Jeru-salem and rejoice over her (13:13-14). Tobit himself blesses God and antici-pates his own happiness if his descendants see the rebuilding of the temple and the renewed glory of the city (13:15-16a). Finally he sings the

cursed be all who hate you and
    speak a harsh word
      against you;
cursed be all who destroy you
    and pull down your walls,
And all who overthrow your
    towers
    and set fire to your homes.
But blessed forever be all those
    who respect you.

¹³Go, then, rejoice and exult over
    the children of the righteous,
for they will all be gathered
    together
and will bless the Lord of the
    ages.
¹⁴Happy are those who love you,
    and happy are those who rejoice
    in your peace.
Happy too are all who grieve
    over all your afflictions,
For they will rejoice over you
    and behold all your joy forever.

¹⁵My soul, bless the Lord, the great
    King;
    ¹⁶for Jerusalem will be rebuilt as
    his house forever.
Happy too will I be if a remnant of
    my offspring survives
    to see your glory and to give
    thanks to the King of
    heaven!

The gates of Jerusalem will be built
    with sapphire and emerald,
    and all your walls with precious
    stones.
The towers of Jerusalem will be
    built with gold,
    and their battlements with
    purest gold.
¹⁷The streets of Jerusalem will be
    paved
    with rubies and stones of Ophir;
¹⁸The gates of Jerusalem will sing
    hymns of gladness,
    and all its houses will cry out,
    Hallelujah!
Blessed be the God of Israel for all
    ages!
For in you the blessed will bless
    the holy name forever and
    ever.

IX. Epilogue

14 **Parting Advice.** ¹So the words of Tobit's hymn of praise came to an end. Tobit died in peace at the age of a hundred and twelve and was buried with honor in Nineveh. ²He was fifty-eight years old when he lost his eyesight, and after he recovered it he lived in prosperity, giving alms; he continued to fear God and give thanks to the divine Majesty.

praises of the new Jerusalem he envisions, and closes as he began, by blessing God (13:16b-18).

EPILOGUE

Tobit 14

Tobit's long life is coming to an end, so he has one more set of instructions for his son, and now he includes his seven grandsons, a perfect number. He begins by predicting the destruction of Nineveh in 612 B.C. and the final defeat of the Assyrians by the Babylonians in 609 B.C. Tobit himself had been taken captive to Nineveh; now he foresees the end of Assyrian

³As he was dying, he summoned his son Tobiah and Tobiah's seven sons, and commanded him, "Son, take your children ⁴and flee into Media, for I believe God's word that Nahum spoke against Nineveh. It will all happen and will overtake Assyria and Nineveh; indeed all that was said by Israel's prophets whom God sent will come to pass. Not one of all their words will remain unfulfilled, but everything will take place in the time appointed for it. So it will be safer in Media than in Assyria or Babylon. For I know and believe that whatever God has said will be accomplished. It will happen, and not a single word of the prophecies will fail.

As for our kindred who dwell in the land of Israel, they will all be scattered and taken into captivity from the good land. All the land of Israel will become a wilderness; even Samaria and Jerusalem will be a wilderness! For a time, the house of God will be desolate and will be burned. ⁵But God will again have mercy on them and bring them back to the land of Israel. They will build the house again, but it will not be like the first until the era when the appointed times will be completed. Afterward all of them will return from their captivity, and they will rebuild Jerusalem with due honor. In it the house of God will also be rebuilt, just as the

power and the rise of the Babylonians who will eventually destroy Jerusalem with its temple and kill many of its inhabitants (587–539 B.C.). He relies on prophetic announcements for this knowledge. Manuscripts differ regarding which prophet he is reading, however. One tradition names the prophet Nahum, who not only foretells the destruction of Nineveh but delights in the rout of this terrible enemy. The other tradition names Jonah, who announces the fall of Nineveh, but who then must endure God's forgiveness and rescue of this hated people. Nahum is the more likely candidate as the original reading, because he is clear about the fall of Nineveh.

Tobit also predicts the return from exile, which begins in 538 B.C., and the rebuilding of the Jerusalem temple, which is dedicated in 516 B.C. Echoing the Deuteronomic theory that the good will be blessed and the wicked punished, he hopes not only for this restoration, however, but envisions that "[a]ll the nations of the world" will worship God in truth and bless God in righteousness (14:6-7). The just will rejoice but the wicked will be wiped out from the land.

Tobit's advice to Tobiah, in the face of the impending disaster, is to return to Media, specifically to Ecbatana, Sarah's home. There he will be sheltered from the upheaval to the west. Tobit also reemphasizes the instructions he gave his son before the first journey to Media. He should remember to give alms, because those who are diligent in this virtue will be saved from death. He tells the story of Ahiqar and his nephew as an example. The nephew, Nadin, tries to kill Ahiqar, who is saved because he gave alms.

prophets of Israel said of it. [6]All the nations of the world will turn and reverence God in truth; all will cast away their idols, which have deceitfully led them into error. [7]They will bless the God of the ages in righteousness. All the Israelites truly mindful of God, who are to be saved in those days, will be gathered together and will come to Jerusalem; in security will they dwell forever in the land of Abraham, which will be given to them. Those who love God sincerely will rejoice, but those who commit sin and wickedness will disappear completely from the land.

[8, 9]"Now, my children, I give you this command: serve God sincerely and do what is pleasing in his sight; you must instruct your children to do what is right and to give alms, to be mindful of God and at all times to bless his name sincerely and with all their strength. Now, as for you, son, leave Nineveh; do not stay here. [10]The day you bury your mother next to me, do not even stay overnight within the confines of the city. For I see that there is much wickedness in it, and much treachery is practiced in it, and people are not ashamed. See, my son, all that Nadin did to Ahiqar, the very one who reared him. Was not Ahiqar brought down alive into the earth? Yet God made Nadin's disgraceful crime rebound against him. Ahiqar came out again into the light, but Nadin went into the everlasting darkness, for he had tried to kill Ahiqar. Because Ahiqar had given alms he escaped from the deadly trap Nadin had set for him. But Nadin fell into the deadly trap himself, and it destroyed him. [11]So, my children, see what almsgiving does, and also what wickedness does—it kills! But now my spirit is about to leave me."

Death of Tobit and Tobiah. They laid him on his bed, and he died; and he was buried with honor. [12]When Tobiah's mother died, he buried her next to his father. He then departed with his wife and children for Media, where he settled in Ecbatana with his father-in-law Raguel. [13]He took respectful care of his aging father-in-law and mother-in-law; and he buried them at Ecbatana in Media. Then he inherited Raguel's estate as well as that of his father Tobit. [14]He died highly respected at the age of one hundred seventeen. [15]But before he died, he saw and heard of the destruction of Nineveh. He saw the inhabitants of the city being led captive into Media by Cyaxares, the king of Media. Tobiah blessed God for all that he had done against the Ninevites and Assyrians. Before dying he rejoiced over Nineveh, and he blessed the Lord God forever and ever.

As is appropriate for the righteous according to Deuteronomy, Tobit lives a long life and dies at the age of 112. He lives long enough to see his predictions fulfilled and blesses God for removing the threat of the Assyrians. Just as the story began with Tobit's care for burying the dead, now Tobit is concerned that Tobiah will bury him and Anna appropriately. The faithful son carries out these instructions and then moves with his family to live with his in-laws. He cares for them in their old age and he buries them with honor as well. Finally he inherits the estates of his father and father-in-law and lives a good life to the age of 117, blessing God "forever and ever."

Judith

Who is Judith? Who is the maid?

Judith is a complex character. Her name means "Jewish/Judean woman," and she acts to deliver the town of Bethulia, which means "virginity." Or is her name taken from the hero, Judas Maccabeus, who delivers the people from the threat of Antiochus Epiphanes (see 1–2 Macc)? Is she modeled on Jael, who hammered a tent peg through the head of the enemy General Sisera (Judg 4:17-22)? Or is she modeled on the earlier deliverer, David, who killed Goliath with a stone and then cut off his head (1 Sam 17:48-51)? Perhaps all of these stories form the portrayal of Judith, who saves her people from destruction at the hands of a terrible enemy.

Judith is a paradoxical character. She takes charge of the situation, assuming a man's role, but she uses feminine wiles to accomplish her task. She is described as a faithful and pious woman, yet she seems aloof from her people, unaware of their distress until it is desperate. She has a maid, who remains nameless and somewhat invisible throughout the story. Is this maid a slave, an indentured servant? Is she a Jew or a Gentile? Is it accurate that Judith "frees" her maid only at the end of her long life? If the maid is Jewish, the law demands that she be freed in the seventh year of her servitude. In any case, the maid is faithful and trustworthy. Judith could not have carried out her daring deed without the essential assistance of the maid.

Judith is not a hero, even though the Jerusalem leaders identify her as such (15:9-10). She consistently names God as the hero who saved the people; she is simply God's servant, who carries out God's plan (13:11-14; 16:5).

Judith also has a rich afterlife. Saint Jerome holds her up as an example for Paula's daughter Eustochium (Ep 22.21.8). Other patristic writers praise her highly, including Clement, Origen, Ambrose, Fulgentius, and Augustine. She becomes a type of Mary and selections from her story appeared in Catholic liturgy before Vatican II for the feasts of the Immaculate Conception and the Assumption. In the current Lectionary a selection from her introduction (8:2-8) is suggested for votive Masses for widows. Artists also delight in painting the scene of Judith's victory over Holofernes. The subjects range from the gory scene of the beheading by Artemisia Gentileschi (1611–12) to the calm and subdued scene of Botticelli's *Return of Judith to Bethulia* (ca. 1472).

Genre and date

The story of Judith is a novella, somewhat longer than a short story and shorter than a novel. The writer has made great efforts to show that this work is fictional. Historical figures are placed in the wrong time and place; historical events are deliberately combined and rearranged. The purpose of the story is not to outline historical facts but to highlight the faithfulness of God who can always be counted on to rescue the people in both ordinary and extraordinary ways.

The book is difficult to date. It was written sometime between the beginning of the Maccabean revolt against the persecution of Antiochus IV Epiphanes (167 B.C.) and the Roman capture of Jerusalem (63 B.C.).

Original language and canonical status

The book of Judith was probably written in Hebrew, although there are no surviving manuscripts in this language. It is one of the few biblical books not found among the Dead Sea Scrolls. Also it was not included in the Hebrew canon, possibly because it was written so late. Thus it is not found in English Bibles from the King James and Revised Standard traditions. It is, however, included in the Septuagint and thus is in the Catholic canon, both Roman and Greek Orthodox. It is also found in the Latin Vulgate thanks to some friends of St. Jerome. He did not intend to include the books not found in the Hebrew canon, but his bishop friends persuaded him to translate Judith and Tobit for them.

Power of prayer

The book of Judith is punctuated by prayer. As soon as the army of Holofernes threatens Bethulia, the people cry out to God and begin to fast (4:9-15). God immediately hears their prayer (4:13), but the people will not know this for many days. In the meantime Achior, expelled by Holofernes, arrives in Bethulia and describes the army's intentions. Immediately the people again turn to prayer (6:18-21). Nonetheless Holofernes besieges the city and the Israelites again cry out to God and blame their leaders (7:19, 29-30). When Judith appears, she exhorts the leaders once more to pray (8:17-26). Then she herself turns to God with a lengthy prayer (9:1-14). As she departs for the Assyrian camp, the leaders bless her and she bows to

God (10:8-9). Even Holofernes praises God, mistakenly thinking God is on his side (11:22-23). Throughout her stay in the camp Judith goes out to the spring to pray with her maid every morning (12:6-8). As she prepares to behead Holofernes, Judith begs God for strength (13:4-7). Then arriving back in Bethulia she encourages the people to praise God for their deliverance (13:11-14, 17-20). The Jerusalem leaders pray a blessing over her (15:9-10). Finally Judith sings a long song of praise (16:1-17). Prayer strengthens all the Israelites. The people are losing hope, but still cling to prayer. Judith never doubts God's presence with her, but prays for courage and the ability to save her people. God hears all their prayers but answers in ways they do not expect.

The prayers are expanded in the Latin Vulgate. The elders not only encourage the people to pray, but add the example of Moses defeating the Amalekites "by holy prayers" (4:12-14, Vulg.). The prayer of the people who have heard Achior's report is also extended (6:14-18, Vulg.). When the people blame the leaders for their distress, they add a prayer of repentance for their sins and beg for mercy (7:19-22, Vulg.).

Who is God?

The central question in this book is "Who is God?" In the early chapters Nebuchadnezzar portrays himself as God, destroying all the gods of the lands he conquers and demanding that all peoples "invoke him as a god" (3:8). Later, in response to Achior's testimony about the God of the Israelites, Holofernes challenges him, "Who is God beside Nebuchadnezzar?" (6:2). For him Nebuchadnezzar is "lord of all the earth," whose words will be effective (6:4). Judith, in her prayer to the Lord, counters Nebuchadnezzar's boasting: "Make every nation and every tribe know clearly that you are God, the God of all power and might" (9:14). Holofernes ironically tells Judith that, if she does what she claims, "your God will be my God" (11:23). Little does he know that he will not have a chance to fulfill that promise. When Judith returns to Bethulia, carrying Holofernes's head, Achior "believed firmly in God," the God of Israel (14:10). In her song, Judith proclaims, "O Lord, great are you and glorious, / marvelous in power and unsurpassable" (16:13). The God of Israel is the one and only God.

Judith

I. Assyrian Threat

Nebuchadnezzar Against Arphaxad. [1]It was the twelfth year of the reign of Nebuchadnezzar, who ruled over the Assyrians in the great city of Nineveh. At that time Arphaxad was ruling over the Medes in Ecbatana. [2]Around Ecbatana he built a wall of hewn stones, three cubits thick and six cubits long. He made the walls seventy cubits high and fifty cubits wide. [3]At its gates he raised towers one hundred cubits high with foundations sixty cubits wide. [4]He made its gates seventy cubits high and forty cubits wide to allow passage of his mighty forces, with his infantry in formation. [5]At that time King Nebuchadnezzar waged war against King Arphaxad in the vast plain that borders Ragau. [6]Rallying to him were all who lived in the hill country, all who lived along the Euphrates, the Tigris, and the Hydaspes, as well as Arioch, king of the Elamites, in the plains. Thus many nations joined the ranks of the Chelodites.

[7]Then Nebuchadnezzar, king of the Assyrians, contacted all the inhabitants of Persia and all who lived in the west,

NEBUCHADNEZZAR'S VICTORY AGAINST ARPHAXAD

Judith 1

This first chapter of Judith suggests that the story is about Nebuchadnezzar rather than the woman for whom the book is named. Nebuchadnezzar seems to have godly power. He summons all the inhabitants of the lands from Persia (modern-day Iran) to the Mediterranean and from the Black Sea to Egypt. When these peoples scorn him, he sets out to destroy them all. The first enemy he confronts and defeats is Arphaxad, ruler of the Medes.

The story seems to be a straightforward tale of kings and battles and greed for power, and it is about all these things. But there are hints already in this first chapter that not everything is what it seems. First of all, there are historical problems. Nebuchadnezzar ruled over Babylon, not Assyria, and his reign was from 605 B.C. to 562 B.C. By the time of his reign Nineveh, the capital of Assyria, was already gone, having been destroyed in 612 B.C. Arphaxad, named here as king of the Medes (1:1), is otherwise unknown,

the inhabitants of Cilicia and Damascus, Lebanon and Antilebanon, and all who lived along the seacoast, ⁸the peoples of Carmel, Gilead, Upper Galilee, and the vast plain of Esdraelon, ⁹and all in Samaria and its cities, and west of the Jordan as far as Jerusalem, Bethany, Chelous, Kadesh, and the river of Egypt; Tahpanhes, Raamses, all the land of Goshen, ¹⁰Tanis, Memphis and beyond, and all the inhabitants of Egypt as far as the borders of Ethiopia.

¹¹But all the inhabitants of the whole land made light of the summons of Nebuchadnezzar, king of the Assyrians, and would not join him in the war. They were not afraid of him, since he was only a single opponent. So they sent back his envoys empty-handed and disgraced. ¹²Then Nebuchadnezzar fell into a violent rage against all the land, and swore by his throne and his kingdom that he would take revenge on all the territories of Cilicia, Damascus, and Syria, and would destroy with his sword all the inhabitants of Moab, Ammon, the whole of Judea, and all those living in Egypt as far as the coasts of the two seas.

Defeat of Arphaxad. ¹³In the seventeenth year he mustered his forces against King Arphaxad and was victorious in his campaign. He routed the whole force of Arphaxad, his entire

but it is worth noting that Assyria was conquered by the Medes and Babylonians, not the other way around.

Exaggeration also characterizes this introductory chapter. The walls Arphaxad builds to defend Ecbatana are, by our measurements, about 105 feet high and 75 feet wide. (A cubit is about 18 inches long.) The stones in the walls are 9 feet long and 4½ feet wide. The towers are 150 feet high and 90 feet wide. Remains of such massive structures would certainly be evident around the area of Ecbatana, but none have been found. The list of peoples summoned by Nebuchadnezzar is also exaggerated. It includes every group living in the Middle East, "the whole land" or "all the land" (a phrase occurring ten times in chs. 1–2). His ambitions include everything from "sea to sea," perhaps the Persian Gulf to the Mediterranean. Finally, in an echo of Artaxerxes's banquet in the book of Esther, Nebuchadnezzar holds a victory banquet lasting a third of a year (see Esth 1:4-5).

The exaggerations and the historical anomalies lead the reader to seek a different purpose for this introduction. What is the author trying to say here? First of all, it is clear that this work is not intended as a historical account, but rather a fictional tale. The confusion of dates and persons must point to another reality. So the second task of the reader is to probe the meaning of these dates and persons. The story opens with the twelfth year of Nebuchadnezzar, 593 B.C. At that time Judah is in trouble. King Jehoiakin and the leading citizens have already been exiled to Babylon. In 593 King Zedekiah, who had been put on the throne by the Babylonians, is invited

cavalry, and all his chariots, ¹⁴and took possession of his cities. He pressed on to Ecbatana, took its towers, sacked its marketplaces, and turned its glory into shame. ¹⁵He captured Arphaxad in the mountains of Ragau, ran him through with spears, and utterly destroyed him once and for all. ¹⁶Then he returned to Nineveh with all his consolidated forces, a very great multitude of warriors; and there he and his forces re-laxed and feasted for one hundred and twenty days.

2 Revenge Planned Against the Western Nations. ¹In the eighteenth year, on the twenty-second day of the first month, there was a discussion in the palace of Nebuchadnezzar, king of the Assyrians, about taking revenge on all the land, as he had threatened. ²He summoned all his attendants and officers, laid before them his secret plan,

to join a coalition against them but refuses. In only a few years, however, Zedekiah changes his position and Nebuchadnezzar besieges and conquers Jerusalem and takes many more people into exile.

The confusion of rulers and their territories also calls up significant events in the people's history. The Assyrians conquered the ten northern tribes, known as Israel, in 722 B.C., deported many of the people, and re-populated the territory with other conquered peoples. The Babylonians under Nebuchadnezzar took the remaining southern tribe, Judah, into exile in 587 B.C. By making Nebuchadnezzar, who was actually the ruler of the Babylonians, the ruler of the Assyrians, the author is suggesting both deportations, the worst tragedies in the people's history. The irony of Nebuchadnezzar's attempt to rule from "sea to sea" is that in the Psalms that phrase describes the rule of the ideal king (Ps 72:8).

REVENGE AGAINST THE WEST AND HOLOFERNES'S CAMPAIGNS

Judith 2

In the eighteenth year of his reign, Nebuchadnezzar constructs his plan to destroy all the peoples who had scorned him. The year is 587 B.C., the year that, in historical fact, Nebuchadnezzar destroyed Jerusalem with its holy temple and took its people into exile. It is the worst year in biblical history for God's people. The date is a warning for the reader to be prepared for disaster—but disaster for whom?

Exaggeration again characterizes the description of Nebuchadnezzar's plan. He will cover the whole land with his soldiers and fill all their watercourses with the dead. He appoints Holofernes as his army commander and commissions him to slaughter and plunder the whole land to the west. So Holofernes sets out with a large force to destroy "all the lands of

and with his own lips recounted in full detail the wickedness of all the land. ³They decided to destroy all who had refused to obey the order he had issued.

⁴When he had fully recounted his plan, Nebuchadnezzar, king of the Assyrians, summoned Holofernes, the ranking general of his forces, second only to himself in command, and said to him: ⁵"Thus says the great king, the lord of all the earth: Go forth from my presence, take with you men of proven valor, one hundred and twenty thousand infantry and twelve thousand cavalry, ⁶and proceed against all the land of the west, because they disobeyed the order I issued. ⁷Tell them to have earth and water ready, for I will come against them in my wrath; I will cover all the land with the feet of my soldiers, to whom I will deliver them as spoils. ⁸Their wounded will fill their ravines

the western region" (2:19). His army is incredibly swift, marching three hundred miles in a mere three days (2:21), and amazingly successful, ravaging every people he encounters.

Throughout this chapter Nebuchadnezzar continues to be described in language usually reserved for God. He calls himself "the great king, the lord of all the earth" (2:5). Psalm 47 describes God with similar phrases: "For the Lord, the Most High, is to be feared, / the great king over all the earth" (Ps 47:3). Psalm 95 declares, "the Lord is the great God, / the great king over all gods" (Ps 95:3), and Jerusalem is called "the city of the great king" (Ps 48:3). In Psalm 97:5 "[t]he mountains melt like wax before the Lord, / before the Lord of all the earth" (see also Ps 97:9). "Fear and dread" of Holofernes, Nebuchadnezzar's army general, fall upon all the peoples of the coastland. In Deuteronomy God promises that "fear and dread" of the Israelites will fall on "the peoples everywhere under heaven" as they march into the Promised Land (Deut 2:25; see Deut 11:25; Josh 2:9).

Nebuchadnezzar declares, "as I live, and by the strength of my kingdom, what I have spoken I will accomplish by my own hand" (Jdt 2:12). But in the prophetic literature, especially at the time of the Babylonian exile, it is God who continually asserts "as I live" (Isa 49:18; Jer 22:24; 46:18; Ezek 5:11; 14:16, 18, 20; 16:48; 17:16, 19; 18:3; 20:3, 31, 33; 33:11, 27; 34:8; 35:6, 11; Zeph 2:9). Deuteronomy also exhorts the people to "observe carefully" all God's commandments (Deut 4:6; 6:25; 7:11; 15:5; 17:10, 19; 19:9; 24:8; 28:1, 13, 15; 29:8; 31:12; 32:46; see Josh 1:8; Neh 10:30; Ezek 43:11). Nebuchadnezzar commands Holofernes, "Do not disobey a single one of the orders of your lord; fulfill them exactly as I have commanded you" (Jdt 2:13).

It seems clear that Nebuchadnezzar is portrayed as a god, using divine language to declare his authority and issue his commands. In Israel's history the exodus from Egypt has been described as a battle between gods.

and wadies, the swelling river will be choked with their dead; ⁹and I will deport them as exiles to the very ends of the earth.

¹⁰"Go before me and take possession of all their territories for me. If they surrender to you, guard them for me until the day of their sentencing. ¹¹As for those who disobey, show them no mercy, but deliver them up to slaughter and plunder in all the land you occupy. ¹²For as I live, and by the strength of my kingdom, what I have spoken I will accomplish by my own hand. ¹³Do not disobey a single one of the orders of your lord; fulfill them exactly as I have commanded you, and do it without delay."

Campaigns of Holofernes. ¹⁴So Holofernes left the presence of his lord, and summoned all the commanders, generals, and officers of the Assyrian forces. ¹⁵He mustered one hundred and twenty thousand picked troops, as his lord had commanded, and twelve thousand mounted archers, ¹⁶and drew them up as a vast force organized for battle. ¹⁷He took along a very large number of camels, donkeys, and mules for carrying their supplies; innumerable sheep, cattle, and goats for their food; ¹⁸abundant provisions for each man, and much gold and silver from the royal palace.

¹⁹Then he and all his forces set out on their expedition in advance of King Nebuchadnezzar, to overrun all the lands of the western region with their chariots, cavalry, and picked infantry. ²⁰A huge, irregular force, too many to count, like locusts, like the dust of the earth, went along with them.

²¹After a three-day march from Nineveh, they reached the plain of Bectileth, and camped opposite Bectileth near the mountains to the north of Upper Cilicia. ²²From there Holofernes took all his forces, the infantry, cavalry, and chariots, and marched into the hill country. ²³He devastated Put and Lud, and plundered all the Rassisites and the Ishmaelites on the border of the wilderness toward the south of the Chelleans.

²⁴Then, following the Euphrates, he went through Mesopotamia, and battered down every fortified city along the Wadi Abron, until he reached the sea. ²⁵He seized the territory of Cilicia, and cut down everyone who resisted him. Then he proceeded to the southern borders of Japheth, toward Arabia. ²⁶He surrounded all the Midianites, burned their tents, and sacked their encampments. ²⁷Descending to the plain of Damascus at the time of the wheat harvest, he set fire to all their fields, destroyed their flocks and herds, looted their cities, devastated their plains, and put all their young men to the sword.

²⁸ Fear and dread of him fell upon all the inhabitants of the coastland, upon

Pharaoh has declared himself a god and YHWH is his opponent. God's people reading the story of Judith will recognize the echoes of that struggle and remember the outcome. Already there are suggestions that this "false god," Nebuchadnezzar, and his general, Holofernes, will never be able to resist the power of the God of Israel.

those in Sidon and Tyre, and those who dwelt in Sur and Ocina, and the inhabitants of Jamnia. Those in Azotus and Ascalon also feared him greatly.

3 **Submission of the Vassal Nations.** ¹So they sent messengers to him to sue for peace in these words: ²"We, the servants of Nebuchadnezzar the great king, lie prostrate before you; do with us as you will. ³See, our dwellings and all our land and every wheat field, our flocks and herds, and all our encampments are at your disposal; make use of them as you please. ⁴Our cities and their inhabitants are also at your service; come and deal with them as you see fit."

⁵After the spokesmen had reached Holofernes and given him this message, ⁶he went down with his forces to the seacoast, stationed garrisons in the fortified cities, and took selected men from them as auxiliaries. ⁷The people of these cities and all the inhabitants of the countryside received him with garlands and dancing to the sound of timbrels. ⁸But he devastated their whole territory and cut down their sacred groves, for he was allowed to destroy all the gods of the land, so that every nation might worship only Nebuchadnezzar, and all their tongues and tribes should invoke him as a god. ⁹At length Holofernes reached Esdraelon in the neighborhood of Dothan, the approach to the main ridge of the Judean mountains; ¹⁰he set up his camp between Geba and Scythopolis, and stayed there a whole month to replenish all the supplies of his forces.

II. Siege of Bethulia

4 **Israel Prepares for War.** ¹When the Israelites who lived in Judea heard of all that Holofernes, the ranking general of Nebuchadnezzar king of the Assyrians, had done to the nations, and how he had looted all their shrines and utterly destroyed them, ²they were in very great fear of him, and greatly alarmed for Jerusalem and the temple of the Lord, their God. ³Now, they had

SUBMISSION OF VASSAL NATIONS AND ISRAEL'S PREPARATION FOR WAR
Judith 3–4

The people of the coastlands, having seen what Holofernes has done to their neighbors, now plead for peace. They offer him everything they have and twice they tell him to do what he pleases (3:2, 4). When Holofernes arrives in their territory with his armies, they welcome him with honor. Will this save them? No! Holofernes destroys their whole territory including their sacred shrines. Nebuchadnezzar must be honored as the only god; all rivals must be deposed (3:8).

Holofernes has now arrived at the edge of Judean territory and is poised to attack, but he delays for a month to restore his troops and supplies. At last we begin to recognize what this story has to do with God's

only recently returned from exile, and all the people of Judea were just now reunited, and the vessels, the altar, and the temple had been purified from profanation. ⁴So they sent word to the whole region of Samaria, to Kona, Bethhoron, Belmain, and Jericho, to Choba and Aesora, and to the valley of Salem. ⁵The people there secured all the high hilltops, fortified the villages on them, and since their fields had recently been harvested, stored up provisions in preparation for war.

⁶Joakim, who was high priest in Jerusalem in those days, wrote to the inhabitants of Bethulia and Betomesthaim, which is opposite Esdraelon, facing the plain near Dothan, ⁷and instructed them to keep firm hold of the mountain passes, since these offered access to Judea. It would be easy to stop those advancing, as the approach was only wide enough for two at a time. ⁸The Israelites carried out the orders given them by Joakim, the high priest, and the senate of the whole people of Israel, in session in Jerusalem.

Israel at Prayer. ⁹All the men of Israel cried to God with great fervor and humbled themselves. ¹⁰They, along with their wives, and children, and domestic animals, every resident alien, hired worker, and purchased slave, girded themselves with sackcloth. ¹¹And all the Israelite men, women, and children who lived in Jerusalem fell

people even though we have not yet met the title character. Once more we have a confusing suggestion of dates (4:2-3). The narrator reports that the people had recently returned from exile, presumably the Babylonian exile. The return from that exile was around 538 B.C., but, as has been already noted, Nebuchadnezzar ruled from 605–562 B.C. and has set out on this campaign to destroy all the nations in 587 B.C., the year the Israelites went into exile. So what the author of this story has done is to combine into one year the people's worst disaster—the deportation in 587 B.C.—and their greatest rescue by God—the return from exile in 538 B.C. So even though a terrible threat looms over them as Holofernes approaches, the reader already knows that they will be saved by God.

So the people begin to prepare for war. They notify the whole region, gather up their resources, and secure the mountain passes. Then they begin the most significant preparation: they fast and pray. They not only put on sackcloth, a sign of penitence, but they even drape the altar in sackcloth. It is as if God is a penitent too! They also remind God that their defeat would result in the profanation of God's own sacred sanctuary. God hears their prayer (4:13). Just as in the book of Tobit (Tob 3:16-17), however, the people do not yet know that God has heard them and is coming to their rescue. It will be some time before they realize that they are saved.

Their cry to God is based on age-old tradition. During their enslavement in Egypt they finally cry out to God and "God heard their moaning

prostrate in front of the temple and sprinkled ashes on their heads, spreading out their sackcloth before the Lord. [12]The altar, too, they draped in sackcloth; and with one accord they cried out fervently to the God of Israel not to allow their children to be seized, their wives to be taken captive, the cities of their inheritance to be ruined, or the sanctuary to be profaned and mocked for the nations to gloat over.

[13]The Lord heard their cry and saw their distress. The people continued fasting for many days throughout Judea and before the sanctuary of the Lord Almighty in Jerusalem. [14]Also girded with sackcloth, Joakim, the high priest, and all the priests in attendance before the Lord, and those who minis-

tered to the Lord offered the daily burnt offering, the votive offerings, and the voluntary offerings of the people. [15]With ashes upon their turbans, they cried to the Lord with all their strength to look with favor on the whole house of Israel.

5 **Achior in the Assyrian War Council.** [1]It was reported to Holofernes, the ranking general of the Assyrian forces, that the Israelites were ready for battle, had blocked the mountain passes, fortified the high hilltops, and placed roadblocks in the plains. [2]In great anger he summoned all the rulers of Moab, the governors of Ammon, and all the satraps of the coastland [3]and said to them: "Now tell me, you Canaanites, what sort of people is this that lives in the hill

and God was mindful of his covenant" (Exod 2:24). Their cry sets in motion the great rescue of the exodus. In the book of Judges over and over the people sin against God and God strengthens their enemies. But when they cry out, God sends a judge to rescue them (see Judg 3:9, 15; 4:3; 6:6-7). Again and again the Psalms assert that when the people cry out, God hears: "On the day I cried out, you answered; / you strengthened my spirit" (Ps 138:3; see Ps 18:7; 22:6, 25; 30:3, 9; 34:7).

We know that God has rescued them before. We know the hope the author has given us through the confusing dates. We know that God has already heard their cry. Yet we must wait to see how God will work the wonder of saving them from this awesome military power at their gates.

ACHIOR IN THE ASSYRIAN WAR COUNCIL

Judith 5

Holofernes is astounded at the audacity of the Israelites, who are preparing to do battle with him. He summons the leaders of the peoples whom he had just recently devastated (Moab, Ammon, and the coastlands) and asks, "what sort of people is this?" His questions are revealing. It is not surprising that he asks, "How large is their force?" But the other questions suggest that Holofernes may unwittingly recognize that he is in

country? Which cities do they inhabit? How large is their force? In what does their power and strength consist? Who has set himself up as their king and the leader of their army? ⁴Why have they alone of all the inhabitants of the west refused to come out to meet me?"

⁵Then Achior, the leader of all the Ammonites, said to him: "My lord, please listen to a report from your servant. I will tell you the truth about this people that lives in the hill country near here. No lie shall escape your servant's lips.

⁶"These people are descendants of the Chaldeans. ⁷They formerly lived in Mesopotamia, for they did not wish to follow the gods of their ancestors who were in the land of the Chaldeans. ⁸Since they abandoned the way of their ancestors, and worshiped the God of heaven, the God whom they had come to know, their ancestors expelled them from the presence of their gods. So they fled to Mesopotamia and lived there a long time. ⁹Their God told them to leave the place where they were living and go to the land of Canaan. Here they

---

more trouble than he realizes. "In what does their power and strength consist?" The story will reveal that their power and strength is in their faith in God. "Who [is] their king?" (5:3). It is the all-powerful God who is their king. If Holofernes heard the true answers to those questions, he would know why these people alone have refused to come out to meet him. He has finally met a power greater than his own.

The person who attempts to reveal this threat to Holofernes is the Ammonite Achior. Achior's name suggests that he is modeled on the wise teacher, Ahiqar, who appears in the book of Tobit (see commentary on Tob 1:21-22; 2:10; 11:18; 14:10), where he is clearly an Israelite. Here he is identified as the leader of the Ammonites, a people said to have descended from Lot's younger daughter (Gen 19:38) and who were enemies of Israel in the pioneer period (see Ps 83:2-8; Deut 23:4-5). Whatever his ancestry, however, Achior clearly understands both the history and the power of the Israelites. He is the ideal person to answer Holofernes's questions.

Although he names no names, Achior's recital of the history begins with Abraham, who, according to Genesis, came from Mesopotamia (Gen 11:27-31). He continues with the story of Joseph and the migration of the whole family of Jacob to Egypt (Gen 37–50). He knows the exodus-wilderness stories and the entrance of the people into the Promised Land. He even moves on to the story of the destruction of Jerusalem in the sixth century and the deportation of the people to Babylon. He ends with the news that the people have returned from exile and restored Jerusalem, possibly the temple as well. In other words, he has summarized in two paragraphs the story of God's people from around the nineteenth century B.C.

settled, and grew very rich in gold, silver, and a great abundance of livestock. [10]Later, when famine had gripped the land of Canaan, they went down into Egypt. They stayed there as long as they found sustenance and there they grew into such a great multitude that the number of their people could not be counted. [11]The king of Egypt, however, rose up against them, and shrewdly forced them to labor at brickmaking; they were oppressed and made into slaves. [12]But they cried to their God, and he struck the whole land of Egypt with plagues for which there was no remedy. So the Egyptians drove them out. [13]Then God dried up the Red Sea before them [14]and led them along the route to Sinai and Kadesh-barnea. They drove out all the inhabitants of the wilderness [15]and settled in the land of the Amorites. By their strength they destroyed all the Heshbonites, crossed the Jordan, and took possession of all the hill country. [16]They drove out before them the Canaanites, the Perizzites, the Jebusites, the Shechemites, and all the Gergesites, and they lived there a long time.

[17]"As long as the Israelites did not sin in the sight of their God, they prospered, for their God, who hates wickedness, was with them. [18]But when they abandoned the way he had prescribed for them, they were utterly destroyed by frequent wars, and finally taken as captives into foreign lands. The temple of their God was razed to the ground, and their cities were occupied by their enemies. [19]But now they have returned to their God, and they have come back from the Diaspora where they were scattered. They have reclaimed Jerusalem, where their sanctuary is, and have settled again in the hill country, because it was unoccupied.

[20]"So now, my master and lord, if these people are inadvertently at fault, or if they are sinning against their God, and if we verify this offense of theirs, then we will be able to go up and conquer them. [21]But if they are not a guilty nation, then let my lord keep his distance; otherwise their Lord and God will shield them, and we will be mocked in the eyes of all the earth."

[22]Now when Achior had finished saying these things, all the people standing round about the tent murmured; and the officers of Holofernes and all the inhabitants of the seacoast and of Moab alike said he should be cut to pieces. [23]"We are not afraid of the Israelites," they said, "for they are a

---

to the sixth century B.C. (Note again the discrepancies with the regnal years of Nebuchadnezzar.)

But Achior knows more than the history. He also understands the theology of this people, particularly Deuteronomic theology. A major principle in the book of Deuteronomy is that if the people are obedient they will be blessed, whereas if they are disobedient they will be punished (see especially Deut 28–29). This principle is the basis of Achior's advice to Holofernes. If these people are sinning, conquering them will not be a problem. But if they are faithful to God, "their Lord and God will shield

powerless people, incapable of a strong defense. [24]Therefore let us attack, master Holofernes. They will become fodder for your great army."

6 [1]When the noise of the crowd surrounding the council had subsided, Holofernes, the ranking general of the Assyrian forces, said to Achior, in the presence of the whole throng of foreigners, of the Moabites, and of the Ammonite mercenaries: [2]"Who are you, Achior and the mercenaries of Ephraim, to prophesy among us as you have done today, and to tell us not to fight against the people of Israel because their God shields them? Who is God beside Nebuchadnezzar? He will

send his force and destroy them from the face of the earth. Their God will not save them; [3]but we, the servants of Nebuchadnezzar, will strike them down with one blow, for they will be unable to withstand the force of our cavalry. [4]We will overwhelm them with it, and their mountains shall be drunk with their blood, and their plains filled with their corpses. Not a trace of them shall survive our attack; they will utterly perish. So says King Nebuchadnezzar, lord of all the earth. For he has spoken, and his words will not be in vain. [5]As for you, Achior, you Ammonite mercenary, for saying these things in a moment of perversity, you will not

them" (Jdt 5:20-21; cf. 5:17-18). The soldiers of Holofernes and all those who heard Achior misjudge the Israelites and encourage Holofernes to attack. They expect an easy victory, but they will be greatly disappointed.

RESPONSE TO ACHIOR AND HIS ARRIVAL IN BETHULIA

Judith 6

Holofernes continues the blasphemy of exalting Nebuchadnezzar as God. He begins by challenging Achior: "Who are you" to speak against Nebuchadnezzar (6:2)? Judith will echo that challenge later in her words to the town elders: "Who are you to put God to the test . . . ?" (8:12), but she is not referring to Nebuchadnezzar but to YHWH. Holofernes clarifies his meaning by adding, "Who is God beside Nebuchadnezzar?" He calls Nebuchadnezzar the "lord of all the earth" and declares that "his words will not be in vain" (6:4). These phrases all suggest divinity. Psalm 97 asserts, "The mountains melt like wax before the LORD, / before the Lord of all the earth" (Ps 97:5; see Zech 6:5). In Isaiah 55 God declares, "So shall my word be / that goes forth from my mouth; / it shall not return to me empty, / but shall do what pleases me, / achieving the end for which I sent it" (Isa 55:11). The question, "Who is God?" continues to move the plot of this story.

Achior is to be tested by the truth of his words. He has said that the Israelites cannot be defeated if they are faithful to God. So Holofernes

see my face after today, until I have taken revenge on this people that came out of Egypt. [6]Then at my return, the sword of my army or the spear of my attendants will pierce your sides, and you will fall among their wounded. [7]My servants will now conduct you to the hill country, and leave you at one of the cities beside the passes. [8]You will not die until you are destroyed together with them. [9]If you still harbor the hope that they will not be taken, then there is no need for you to be downcast. I have spoken, and not one of my words will fail to be fulfilled."

[10]Then Holofernes ordered the servants who were standing by in his tent to seize Achior, conduct him to Bethulia, and hand him over to the Israelites. [11]So the servants seized him and took him out of the camp into the plain. From the plain they led him up into the hill country until they reached the springs below Bethulia.

[12]When the men of the city saw them, they seized their weapons and ran out of the city to the top of the hill, and all the slingers kept them from coming up by hurling stones at them. [13]So, taking cover below the hill, they bound Achior and left him lying at the foot of the hill; then they returned to their lord.

Achior in Bethulia. [14]The Israelites came down from their city and found him, untied him, and brought him into Bethulia. They placed him before the rulers of the city, [15]who in those days were Uzziah, son of Micah of the tribe of Simeon, and Chabris, son of Gothoniel, and Charmis, son of Melchiel. [16]They then convened all the elders of the city, and all their young men, as well as the women, gathered in haste at the place of assembly. They placed Achior in the center of the people, and Uzziah questioned him about what had happened. [17]He replied by giving them an account of what was said in the council of Holofernes, and of all his own words among the Assyrian rulers, and of all the boasting threats of Holofernes against the house of Israel.

[18]At this the people fell prostrate and worshiped God, and they cried

---

sends him to Bethulia to experience whatever its citizens experience. Holofernes taunts him that he should not be downcast, but ironically Holofernes is correct. Achior is much better off with the people of Bethulia than with the army of Holofernes. He is left bound at the foot of the hill in front of Bethulia where the Israelites find him. They convene the city council and question him about what is happening in Holofernes's camp. Thus he becomes an asset to Bethulia, although its people do not know that yet.

The people's first response is to turn to God in prayer. They know where their power lies, as indeed Achior has stated. They contrast their humility with the arrogance of Holofernes and his army and beg for God's mercy. Then Uzziah holds a banquet for the elders with Achior as the honored guest. The banquet is in marked contrast to the situation that will

out: [19]"Lord, God of heaven, look at their arrogance! Have mercy on our people in their abject state, and look with favor this day on the faces of those who are consecrated to you." [20]Then they reassured Achior and praised him highly. [21]Uzziah brought him from the place of assembly to his home, where he gave a banquet for the elders. That whole night they called upon the God of Israel for help.

The Campaign Against Israel [1]The following day Holofernes ordered his whole army, and all the troops who had come to join him, to break camp and move against Bethulia, seize the passes into the hills, and make war on the Israelites. [2]That same day all their fighting men went into action. Their forces numbered a hundred and sev-

enty thousand infantry and twelve thousand cavalry, not counting the baggage train or the men who accompanied it on foot, a very great army. [3]They encamped at the spring in the valley near Bethulia, and spread crosswise toward Dothan as far as Balbaim, and lengthwise from Bethulia to Cyamon, which faces Esdraelon.

[4]When the Israelites saw how many there were, they were greatly distressed and said to one another, "Soon they will strip the whole land bare. Neither the high mountains nor the valleys nor the hills will bear their weight." [5]Yet they all seized their weapons, lighted fires on their towers, and kept watch throughout the night.

The Siege of Bethulia. [6]On the second day Holofernes led out all his cavalry

soon face the Israelites as they suffer the effects of Holofernes's siege. But on this night they have confidence in God's rescue even as they continue to pray until morning.

THE SIEGE OF BETHULIA

Judith 7

Holofernes now musters his whole army to move against the little town of Bethulia, the only place that has refused to surrender to him. His army, made up of his own forces plus those of the peoples who have joined him, consists of 182,000 soldiers, not counting the support troops. This force is only slightly larger than the number of Allied troops who landed at Normandy on D-Day, June 6, 1944. That force numbered 160,000. The extent of the encampment of Holofernes's army is impossible to determine, since Bethulia itself appears nowhere outside the book of Judith. The locations of Balbaim and Cyamon are also unknown. The geographic data may well be an invention of the author whose intent is clearly to demonstrate that the threat against this little town is immense.

The Israelites' immediate neighbors to the south, Edomites and Moabites, as well as the generals of the coastal region suggest a plan to

in the sight of the Israelites who were in Bethulia. [7]He reconnoitered the ascents to their city and located their springs of water; these he seized, stationing armed detachments around them, while he himself returned to his troops.

[8]All the rulers of the Edomites, all the leaders of the Moabites, together with the generals of the coastal region, came to Holofernes and said: [9]"Master, please listen to what we have to say, that there may be no losses among your forces. [10]These Israelite troops do not rely on their spears, but on the height of the mountains where they dwell, for it is not easy to reach the summit of their mountains. [11]Therefore, master, do not attack them in regular formation, and not a single one of your troops will fall. [12]Stay in your camp, and spare every man of your force. Have some of your servants keep control of the spring of water that flows out at the base of the mountain, [13]for that is where the inhabitants of Bethulia get their water. Then thirst will destroy them, and they will surrender their city. Meanwhile, we and our troops will go up to the nearby hilltops and encamp there to guard against anyone's leaving the city. [14]They and their wives and children will languish with hunger, and even before the sword strikes them they will be laid low in the streets where they live. [15]Thus you will render them dire punishment for their rebellion and their refusal to meet you peaceably."

[16]Their words pleased Holofernes and all his attendants, and he ordered their proposal to be carried out. [17]So the Ammonites moved camp, together with five thousand Assyrians. They encamped in the valley and held the water supply and the springs of the Israelites. [18]The Edomites and the Ammonites went up and encamped in the hill country opposite Dothan; and they sent some of their men to the southeast

---

Holofernes by which he can conquer Bethulia without losing a single soldier. Israel's troubled history with the Edomites and Moabites goes back to the pioneer period when the people were entering the land under the direction of Joshua. The Edomites refused to allow the Israelites to go through their territory (Num 20:14-21), and the Moabite king hired the prophet Balaam to curse the Israelites, which he was unable to do (Num 22–25). Now the Edomites and Moabites advise Holofernes to weaken the people of Bethulia by cutting off their access to water. All the besieging army needs to do is wait. Holofernes agrees to the plan and the siege begins. The local armies of Edomites and Ammonites guard the springs and the hills surrounding Bethulia.

At this point in the story (7:19) the focus moves from Holofernes's camp to the town of Bethulia. As Achior warned Holofernes, the Israelites immediately turn to God. They knew, as Esther knew, that they have no help but God (Esth 14:3[C14]; 14:14[C:25]). But after thirty-four days, when they have no water and people are collapsing from thirst, they go to

opposite Egrebel, near Chusi, which is on Wadi Mochmur. The rest of the Assyrian army was encamped in the plain, covering all the land. Their tents and equipment were spread out in profusion everywhere, and they formed a vast multitude.

The Distress of the Israelites. ¹⁹The Israelites cried to the Lord, their God, for they were disheartened, since all their enemies had them surrounded, and there was no way of escaping from them. ²⁰The whole Assyrian army, infantry, chariots, and cavalry, kept them thus surrounded for thirty-four days. All the reservoirs of water failed the inhabitants of Bethulia, ²¹and the cisterns ran dry, so that on no day did they have enough water to drink, for their drinking water was rationed. ²²Their children were listless, and the women and youths were fainting from thirst and were collapsing in the streets and gateways of the city, with no strength left in them.

²³So all the people, including youths, women, and children, went in a crowd to Uzziah and the rulers of the city. They cried out loudly and said before all the elders: ²⁴"May God judge between you and us! You have done us grave injustice in not making peace with the Assyrians. ²⁵There is no one to help us now! God has sold us into their hands by laying us prostrate before them in thirst and utter exhaustion. ²⁶So now, summon them and deliver the whole city as plunder to the troops of Holofernes and to all his forces; ²⁷we would be better off to become their prey. Although we would be made slaves, at least we would live, and not have to see our little ones dying before our eyes, and our wives and children breathing their last. ²⁸We adjure you by heaven and earth and by our God, the Lord of our ancestors, who is punishing us for our sins and the sins of our ancestors, that this very day you do as we have proposed."

the elders of the city and beg them to make peace with the Assyrians. They consider themselves to be in the same situation as their ancestors in the settlement period who, when they sinned, were "sold" by God to their enemies (Judg 2:14; 3:8; 4:2; 10:7; cf. Esth 7:4). As Esther argued before Ahasuerus, it would be better to be slaves than for all the people to die (Esth 7:4). They blame Uzziah, the leader, just as their ancestors blamed Moses: "You have made us offensive to Pharaoh and his servants, putting a sword into their hands to kill us" (Exod 5:21). Uzziah pledges to do as they say, but only after waiting five more days. God now has a time limit to deliver the people.

Thirty-four days seems a strange number for the end of the people's patience. Is there more significance to this number? It is one shy of a multiple of seven, a perfect number. Does this suggest that it is not quite God's time yet? The thirty-four days also match the time of God's rescue: Judith will spend four days in the Assyrian camp and after Holofernes's death the Israelites will spend thirty days plundering that camp.

²⁹All in the assembly with one accord broke into shrill wailing and cried loudly to the Lord their God. ³⁰But Uzziah said to them, "Courage, my brothers and sisters! Let us endure patiently five days more for the Lord our God to show mercy toward us; for God will not utterly forsake us. ³¹But if these days pass and help does not come to us, I will do as you say." ³²Then he dismissed the people. The men returned to their posts on the walls and towers of the city, the women and children went back to their homes. Throughout the city they were in great misery.

III. Judith, Instrument of the Lord

Description of Judith. ¹Now in those days Judith, daughter of Merari, son of Ox, son of Joseph, son of Oziel, son of Elkiah, son of Ananias, son of Gideon, son of Raphain, son of Ahitub, son of Elijah, son of Hilkiah, son of Eliab, son of Nathanael, son of Salamiel, son of Sarasadai, son of Simeon, son of Israel, heard of this. ²Her husband, Manasseh, of her own tribe and clan, had died at the time of the barley harvest. ³While he was supervising those who bound the sheaves in the field, he was overcome by the heat; and he collapsed on his bed and died in Bethulia, his native city. He was buried with his ancestors in the field between Dothan and Balamon. ⁴ Judith was living as a widow in her home for three years and four months. ⁵She set up a tent for herself on the roof of her house, put sackcloth about her waist, and wore widow's clothing. ⁶She fasted all the days of her widowhood, except sabbath eves and sabbaths, new moon eves and new moons, feastdays and holidays of the house of Israel. ⁷She was beautiful in appearance and very lovely to behold. Her husband, Manasseh, had left her gold and silver, male and female servants, livestock and fields,

ARRIVAL OF JUDITH AND HER RESPONSE TO THE CRISIS

Judith 8

Finally, after seven chapters setting the stage, we meet the title character of this book. Her introduction is impressive. She is given a sixteen-member genealogy, tracing her ancestry all the way back to Jacob/Israel. Rarely are genealogies given for women in the Old Testament and this one is certainly the most impressive. A second bit of information concerning her identity is that her marriage was endogamous, that is, her husband was from her own clan. This practice was common in the late Old Testament period (see Tob 1:9; 4:12-13). Thirdly, she has been a widow for forty months. But she is also a rarity in this category. Widows did not generally inherit their husband's property; it went to other male members of the clan. Widows are among the most vulnerable persons in society along with Levites, resident aliens, and orphans; faithful people are exhorted to support them (see Exod 22:21-22; Deut 14:29; 24:17-21; 26:12-13; 27:19). But

which she was maintaining. [8]No one had a bad word to say about her, for she feared God greatly.

Judith and the Elders. [9]So when Judith heard of the harsh words that the people, discouraged by their lack of water, had spoken against their ruler, and of all that Uzziah had said to them in reply, swearing that he would hand over the city to the Assyrians at the end of five days, [10]she sent her maid who was in charge of all her things to summon Uzziah, Chabris, and Charmis, the elders of her city. [11]When they came, she said to them: "Listen to me, you rulers of the people of Bethulia. What you said to the people today is not right. You pronounced this oath, made between God and yourselves, and promised to hand over the city to our enemies unless within a certain time the Lord comes to our aid. [12]Who are you to put God to the test today, setting yourselves in the place of God in human affairs? [13]And now it is the Lord Almighty you are putting to the test, but you will never understand anything! [14]You cannot plumb the depths of the human heart or grasp the workings of the human mind; how then can you fathom God, who has made all these things, or discern his mind, or understand his plan?

"No, my brothers, do not anger the Lord our God. [15]For if he does not plan to come to our aid within the five days, he has it equally within his power to protect us at such time as he pleases, or to destroy us in the sight of our enemies. [16]Do not impose conditions on the plans of the Lord our God. God is not like a human being to be moved by threats, nor like a mortal to be cajoled.

[17]"So while we wait for the salvation that comes from him, let us call upon him to help us, and he will hear our cry if it pleases him. [18]For there has not risen among us in recent generations,

---

Judith has inherited her husband's property, and she is very wealthy. A characteristic that will become important as the story continues is that she is also very beautiful.

More important than her external characteristics, however, is her internal character. Judith is a very pious and God-fearing woman. She is faithful to the liturgical calendar of feasts and holidays, but on all other days she fasts and wears sackcloth, a penitential garment. She is highly respected in Bethulia. But she is not a shy, retiring hermit. She feels free to summon the leaders of the city and to scold them for their lack of faith. In a surprising reversal she teaches them the ways of God and warns them not to pretend to limit God's power or freedom. She reiterates the Deuteronomic theory of retribution, but asserts that she knows they have been faithful to God, so God will certainly rescue them. She warns that they themselves will be blamed if Bethulia falls and all Judea after it. Finally she gives the leaders advice: wait for God's salvation, call on God for help, set an example for the common people, and even thank God for putting

nor does there exist today, any tribe, or clan, or district, or city of ours that worships gods made by hands, as happened in former days. [19]It was for such conduct that our ancestors were handed over to the sword and to pillage, and fell with great destruction before our enemies. [20]But since we acknowledge no other god but the Lord, we hope that he will not disdain us or any of our people. [21]If we are taken, then all Judea will fall, our sanctuary will be plundered, and God will demand an account from us for their profanation. [22]For the slaughter of our kindred, for the taking of exiles from the land, and for the devastation of our inheritance, he will hold us responsible among the nations. Wherever we are enslaved, we will be a scandal and a reproach in the eyes of our masters. [23]Our servitude will not work to our advantage, but the Lord our God will turn it to disgrace.

[24]"Therefore, my brothers, let us set an example for our kindred. Their lives depend on us, and the defense of the sanctuary, the temple, and the altar rests with us. [25]Besides all this, let us give thanks to the Lord our God for putting us to the test as he did our ancestors. [26]Recall how he dealt with Abraham, and how he tested Isaac, and all that happened to Jacob in Syrian Mesopotamia while he was tending the flocks of Laban, his mother's brother. [27]He has not tested us with fire, as he did them, to try their hearts, nor is he taking vengeance on us. But the Lord chastises those who are close to him in order to admonish them."

[28]Then Uzziah said to her: "All that you have said you have spoken truthfully, and no one can deny your words. [29]For today is not the first time your wisdom has been evident, but from your earliest days all the people have recognized your understanding, for your heart's disposition is right. [30]The people, however, were so thirsty that they forced us to do for them as we have promised, and to bind ourselves by an oath that we cannot break. [31]But now, since you are a devout woman,

them to the test. To support her argument she recites their history, beginning with Abraham. She is a fearless woman.

Uzziah acknowledges her wisdom and her piety, but has no imagination that God will save them in any other way than by sending rain. He dismisses Judith's strength and, in effect, pats her on the head and says, "We know you are a good woman. Go home and pray for rain." But Judith has other plans that neither Uzziah nor the reader suspect. Uzziah has not realized that she has included herself with the leaders by saying, "let *us* set an example" (8:24, emphasis added). She announces that she has a plan that will astonish everyone and again gives instructions to Uzziah and the leaders to do what she says. Uzziah's time limit for God will be upheld and he will not be embarrassed. But their rescue will come in a way he cannot imagine. Judith is not a woman to be dismissed easily.

pray for us that the Lord may send rain to fill up our cisterns. Then we will no longer be fainting from thirst."

³²Then Judith said to them: "Listen to me! I will perform a deed that will go down from generation to generation among our descendants. ³³Stand at the city gate tonight to let me pass through with my maid; and within the days you have specified before you will surrender the city to our enemies, the Lord will deliver Israel by my hand. ³⁴You must not inquire into the affair, for I will not tell you what I am doing until it has been accomplished." ³⁵Uzziah

and the rulers said to her, "Go in peace, and may the Lord God go before you to take vengeance upon our enemies!" ³⁶Then they withdrew from the tent and returned to their posts.

The Prayer of Judith. ¹Judith fell prostrate, put ashes upon her head, and uncovered the sackcloth she was wearing. Just as the evening incense was being offered in the temple of God in Jerusalem, Judith cried loudly to the Lord: ²"Lord, God of my father Simeon, ▶ into whose hand you put a sword to take revenge upon the foreigners who had defiled a virgin by violating her,

But there are also problems in this scenario. Why, when this mortal threat to the city has been going on for days, does she seem to have just heard of it? Does she not know about the lack of water? Where is she getting water? She exhorts the leaders to call upon God, but they have been doing that for days already. Is she so isolated on her rooftop that she is unaware of the terrible distress of her fellow townspeople? Has her maid not brought her any news until this day? The reader is challenged to accept these contradictions and submit to the flow of the story.

THE PRAYER OF JUDITH

Judith 9

Judith follows the accepted ritual for prayer in the postexilic period. Like Esther's uncle Mordecai, she wears sackcloth and ashes (Esth 4:1; see Esth 4:3; 1 Macc 3:47; Dan 9:3). Like Daniel and Ezra, she prays at the time of the evening offering (Ezra 9:5; Dan 9:21; 2 Chr 13:11; 1 Macc 4:50; 2 Macc 10:3; see Exod 30:8). But her prayer indicates the violence she intends to do. She begins by telling the story of her ancestor Simeon, one of Jacob's sons. When Jacob's daughter Dinah went out to visit the neighboring women, she had sexual relations with Shechem, the son of the region's leader (Gen 34). Hamor, Shechem's father, went to discuss the matter with Jacob, hoping to make peace by proposing that Shechem marry Dinah. But Dinah's full brothers, Simeon and Levi, have a more sinister plan. They demand that all the men of Hamor's clan be circumcised. Then, when the men are weakened and in pain, Simeon and Levi massacre all of

78

▶ This symbol indicates a cross reference number in the *Catechism of the Catholic Church*. See page 103 for number citations.

shaming her by uncovering her thighs, and dishonoring her by polluting her womb. You said, 'This shall not be done!' Yet they did it. ³Therefore you handed over their rulers to slaughter; and you handed over to bloodshed the bed in which they lay deceived, the same bed that had felt the shame of their own deceiving. You struck down the slaves together with their masters, and the masters upon their thrones. ⁴Their wives you handed over to plunder, and their daughters to captivity, and all the spoils you divided among your favored children, who burned with zeal for you and in their abhorrence of the defilement of their blood called on you for help. O God, my God, hear me also, a widow.

⁵"It is you who were the author of those events and of what preceded and followed them. The present and the future you have also planned. Whatever you devise comes into being. ⁶The things you decide come forward and say, 'Here we are!' All your ways are in readiness, and your judgment is made with foreknowledge.

⁷"Here are the Assyrians, a vast force, priding themselves on horse and chariot, boasting of the power of their infantry, trusting in shield and spear, bow and sling. They do not know that you are the Lord who crushes wars; ⁸Lord is your name. Shatter their strength in your might, and crush their force in your wrath. For they have resolved to profane your sanctuary, to defile the tent where your glorious name resides, and to break off the horns of your altar with the sword. ⁹See their pride, and send forth your fury upon their heads. Give me, a widow, a strong hand to execute my plan. ¹⁰By the deceit of my lips, strike down slave together with ruler, and ruler together

them and take all their possessions including their wives and daughters. Judith speaks admiringly of their action and declares that it was God who inspired it. She will also give God credit for what she plans to do.

She describes the pride of the Assyrians and their ignorance of God's power. She echoes the song of Miriam and Moses in Exodus 15, declaring that the Assyrians think their horses and chariots will save them when, in fact, the Lord is the one "who crushes wars" (Jdt 9:7; Exod 15:1-3, 21; Ps 46:9-10; 76:4-5). She is equating this rescue of God's people with their most central event, the exodus. She gives God reasons to destroy these enemies. God must protect the holiness of the sanctuary, the place where God's name resides. God is also the protector of the lowly and weak. She names all the titles for God that she knows (9:12). She declares that no one can save her people but the Lord. She has persuaded the elders of Bethulia; now she is using everything she can in order to persuade God.

She asks for two things for herself: a strong hand and deceitful lips. She will indeed deceive Holofernes, often by telling the truth, but telling it in such a way that he misunderstands her. Her strong hand will not only

with attendant. Crush their arrogance by the hand of a female.

[11]"Your strength is not in numbers, nor does your might depend upon the powerful. You are God of the lowly, helper of those of little account, supporter of the weak, protector of those in despair, savior of those without hope.

[12]"Please, please, God of my father, God of the heritage of Israel, Master of heaven and earth, Creator of the waters, King of all you have created, hear my prayer! [13]Let my deceitful words wound and bruise those who have planned dire things against your covenant, your holy temple, Mount Zion, and the house your children possess. [14]Make every nation and every tribe know clearly that you are God, the God of all power and might, and that there is no other who shields the people of Israel but you alone."

10 **Judith Prepares to Depart.** [1]As soon as Judith had ceased her prayer to the God of Israel and finished all these words, [2]she rose from the ground. She called her maid and they went down into the house, which she used only on sabbaths and feast days. [3]She took off the sackcloth she had on, laid aside the garments of her widowhood, washed her body with water, and anointed herself with rich ointment. She arranged her hair, put on a diadem, and dressed in the festive attire she had worn while her husband, Manasseh, was living. [4]She chose sandals for her feet, and put on her anklets,

---

kill Holofernes, but it will shame him and all the Assyrians. To be defeated by the hand of a female is the height of disgrace. To emphasize this point, she does not use the word for "woman" (*gyne*) in verse 10, but the generic word for "female" (*theleia*).

JUDITH AND HER MAID GO OUT TO WAR

Judith 10

Now that she has completed her prayer, the most important part of her plan, Judith goes on to make other preparations for battle. Her weapons are beauty and wit (cf. Esth 15:5[D:5]); she intends to entice Holofernes and all his soldiers. Her ritual is careful and thorough, from inside to outside. (Again it is puzzling where she got the water to bathe.) The narrator cannot stop repeating the success of her efforts. The elders are amazed at her beauty (10:7). The Assyrian guards are so impressed that they send a hundred men to escort her to Holofernes (10:14-15). All the men in the Assyrian camp are astounded at her beauty. Paradoxically they exclaim that all the men of her people should be killed since they have the power to outwit the whole world (10:19). Even Holofernes and his attendants are awestruck by her appearance (10:23). They will all soon discover to their dismay that even one Israelite woman has the power to outwit all their might!

bracelets, rings, earrings, and all her other jewelry. Thus she made herself very beautiful, to entice the eyes of all the men who should see her.

[5]She gave her maid a skin of wine and a jug of oil. She filled a bag with roasted grain, dried fig cakes, and pure bread. She wrapped all her dishes and gave them to the maid to carry.

[6]Then they went out to the gate of the city of Bethulia and found Uzziah and the elders of the city, Chabris and Charmis, standing there. [7]When they saw Judith transformed in looks and differently dressed, they were very much astounded at her beauty and said to her, [8]"May the God of our ancestors grant you favor and make your design successful, for the glory of the Israelites and the exaltation of Jerusalem." [9]Judith bowed down to God.

Judith and Her Maid Leave Bethulia. Then she said to them, "Order the gate of the city opened for me, that I may go to accomplish the matters we discussed." So they ordered the young men to open the gate for her, as she had requested, [10]and they did so. Then Judith and her maidservant went out. The men of the city kept her in view as she went down the mountain and crossed the valley; then they lost sight of her.

IV. Judith Goes Out To War

[11]As Judith and her maid walked directly across the valley, they encountered the Assyrian patrol. [12]The men took her in custody and asked her, "To what people do you belong? Where do you come from, and where are you going?" She replied: "I am a daughter of the Hebrews, and I am fleeing from them, because they are about to be delivered up to you as prey. [13]I have come to see Holofernes, the ranking general of your forces, to give him a trustworthy report; in his presence I will show him the way by which he can ascend and take possession of the whole hill country without a single one of his men suffering injury or loss of life."

[14]When the men heard her words and gazed upon her face, which appeared marvelously beautiful to them, they said to her, [15]"By hastening down to see our master, you have saved your

---

Beauty is not Judith's only weapon. She plans carefully. She takes food that she can eat in accordance with kosher laws. She will use another religious ritual, daily purification with water, to ensure her escape route (12:7). More importantly, she takes her faithful maid, who will assist her in her plot. The maid is successful at remaining invisible. When the two women leave Bethulia and cross the valley, the men keep only Judith ("her," 10:10) in view. When the two women meet the Assyrian patrol, they take "her" into custody (10:12). The hundred men escort both women to Holofernes's tent, but the news in the camp is of "her" arrival (10:17-18). Holofernes is informed about "her" and the attendants usher "her" into the tent (10:18-20). Presumably at this point the maid remains outside the tent, but she is still unnoticed. This invisibility makes it possible for the maid to be not only a companion for Judith, but a sentinel outside Holofernes's tent.

life. Now go to his tent; some of us will accompany you to hand you over to him. ¹⁶When you stand before him, have no fear in your heart; give him the report you have given us, and he will treat you well." ¹⁷So they selected a hundred of their men as an escort for her and her maid, and these conducted them to the tent of Holofernes.

¹⁸As the news of her arrival spread among the tents, a crowd gathered in the camp. They came and stood around her as she waited outside the tent of Holofernes, while he was being informed about her. ¹⁹They marveled at her beauty, regarding the Israelites with wonder because of her, and they said to one another, "Who can despise this people who have such women among them? It is not good to leave one of their

men alive, for if any were to be spared they could beguile the whole earth."

Judith Meets Holofernes. ²⁰Then the guards of Holofernes and all his attendants came out and ushered her into the tent. ²¹Holofernes was reclining on his bed under a canopy woven of purple, gold, emeralds, and other precious stones. ²²When they announced her to him, he came out to the front part of the tent, preceded by silver lamps. ²³When Judith came before Holofernes and his attendants, they all marveled at the beauty of her face. She fell prostrate and paid homage to him, but his servants raised her up.

11 ¹Then Holofernes said to her: "Take courage, woman! Have no fear in your heart! I have never harmed anyone who chose to serve

Judith begins her strategy of deceit as soon as she meets the Assyrian patrol (10:12-13). She is not fleeing from her people. (She calls them "Hebrews," a term sometimes used by foreigners for the Israelites; see Gen 40:15; 43:32; Exod 2:6, 13.) They are not "about to be delivered up." It is the Assyrians who will be delivered up. She is not going to give Holofernes a "trustworthy report." He will not "take possession of the whole hill country," and his men will be killed and the survivors will flee for their lives. The only true sentence she utters is, "I have come to see Holofernes" (10:13).

Before Judith set out, she prostrated before God and prayed. When she is brought into the presence of Holofernes, she again falls prostrate and pays homage. Her motive, however, is far different this second time. She will do everything she can to encourage Holofernes in the misperception that he has absolute power and is the total focus of her attention.

JUDITH AND HOLOFERNES

Judith 11

When Judith comes into Holofernes's presence, he says at the beginning and end of his speech, "Take courage" (Greek *tharseo*, 11:1, 3). It is the same word that Uzziah used in encouraging the people to hold out for

Nebuchadnezzar, king of all the earth. ²As for your people who live in the hill country, I would never have raised my spear against them, had they not insulted me. They have brought this upon themselves. ³But now tell me why you have fled from them and come to us? In any case, you have come to safety. Take courage! Your life is spared tonight and for the future. ⁴No one at all will harm you. Rather, you will be well treated, as are the servants of my lord, King Nebuchadnezzar."

⁵Judith answered him: "Listen to the words of your servant, and let your maidservant speak in your presence! I will say nothing false to my lord this night. ⁶If you follow the words of your maidservant, God will successfully perform a deed through you, and my lord will not fail to achieve his designs. ⁷I swear by the life of Nebuchadnezzar, king of all the earth, and by the power of him who has sent you to guide all living things, that not only do human beings serve him through you; but even the wild animals, and the cattle, and the birds of the air, because of your strength, will live for Nebuchadnezzar and his whole house. ⁸Indeed, we have heard of your wisdom and cleverness. The whole earth is aware that you above all others in the kingdom are able, rich in experience, and distinguished in military strategy.

⁹"As for Achior's speech in your council, we have heard it. When the men of Bethulia rescued him, he told

five more days (7:30). This word is common in the postexilic novellas. In the book of Tobit Raphael twice tells the blind Tobit to "take courage" (Tob 5:10). Sarah's mother encourages her daughter twice before her wedding with Tobiah (7:17). Sarah's father, Raguel, echoes his wife in encouraging the young people as they return to Tobiah's family (8:21). Finally Tobiah says, "Courage, father" to Tobit as he applies the fish gall that will remove his blindness (11:11). In the Greek additions to Esther, Ahasuerus revives Esther from her faint by saying, "Take courage" (Esth 15:9 [D:9]). By contrast, the word appears only four times in the rest of the Old Testament (Gen 35:17; Exod 14:13; 20:20; 1 Kgs 17:13). Courage is clearly a necessary virtue for the Jews in the late postexilic period.

Judith's conversation with Holofernes is a study in the advice a nineteenth-century poet gave: "Tell all the truth but tell it slant" (Emily Dickinson). She declares that she will "say nothing false to [her] lord." She also asserts that her lord "will not fail to achieve his designs" (11:5-6). Holofernes assumes that he is "her lord," but the reader suspects it is the Lord God. When she states that she swears by Nebuchadnezzar's life and by the power of the one who has sent Holofernes to guide all living things, the reader is certain that she has her fingers crossed behind her back. Everything she says in this first speech can be applied to the Lord God, and it is virtually certain that this is the power Judith has in mind. Judith

them all he had said to you. ¹⁰So then, my lord and master, do not disregard his word, but bear it in mind, for it is true. Indeed our people are not punished, nor does the sword prevail against them, except when they sin against their God. ¹¹But now their sin has caught up with them, by which they will bring the wrath of their God upon them when they do wrong; so that my lord will not be repulsed and fail, but death will overtake them. ¹²Because their food has given out and all their water is running low, they have decided to kill their animals, and are determined to consume all the things which God in his laws has forbidden them to eat. ¹³They have decided that they would use the first fruits of grain and the tithes of wine and oil, which they had consecrated and reserved for the priests who minister in the presence of our God in Jerusalem—things which the people should not so much as touch with their hands. ¹⁴They have sent messengers to Jerusalem to bring back permission from the senate, for even there people have done these things. ¹⁵On the very day when the response reaches them and they act upon it, they will be handed over to you for destruction.

¹⁶"As soon as I, your servant, learned all this, I fled from them. God has sent me to perform with you such deeds as will astonish people throughout the whole earth who hear of them. ¹⁷Your servant is, indeed, a God-fearing woman, serving the God of heaven night and day. Now I will remain with you, my lord; but each night your

---

is deceiving Holofernes, but she is doing it with a mixture of truth and falsehood and flattery. In his pride Holofernes misses the irony and this failure will bring his demise.

Judith then turns to Achior's speech and declares truly that Achior is correct about the Deuteronomic theory that the good are blessed and the wicked punished. But then she states falsely that the people have sinned or are planning to sin by eating forbidden food. She has no evidence that this is true and she herself is very careful to observe these same dietary laws. It is false also that she has fled from her people, but it is true that God has sent her to perform amazing deeds (11:16). It is no wonder that Holofernes is confused! Unwittingly he even begins to mix truth and falsity. He is correct that God has done well in sending Judith and that destruction will come to those who have despised the true Lord, but he is fatally wrong that the victory will come to him (11:21-22). It is true that Judith will be renowned, but false that she will live in Nebuchadnezzar's palace (11:23).

Judith is not only focused on deceiving Holofernes in this encounter. She also sets up her escape route. Having convinced the general that she is on his side, she describes her piety to him. She says truly that she is a God-fearing woman; she serves "the God of heaven night and day." So she

servant will go out into the valley and pray to God. He will tell me when they have committed their offenses. ¹⁸Then I will come and let you know, so that you may march out with all your forces, and not one of them will be able to withstand you. ¹⁹I will lead you through the heart of Judea until you come to Jerusalem, and there in its center I will set up your throne. You will drive them like sheep that have no shepherd, and not even a dog will growl at you. This was told to me in advance and announced to me, and I have been sent to tell you."

²⁰Her words pleased Holofernes and all his attendants. They marveled at her wisdom and exclaimed, ²¹"No other woman from one end of the earth to the other looks so beautiful and speaks so wisely!" ²²Then Holofernes said to her: "God has done well in sending you ahead of your people, to bring victory to our hands, and destruction to those who have despised my lord. ²³You are not only beautiful in appearance, but you are also eloquent. If you do as you have said, your God will be my God; you will live in the palace of King Nebuchadnezzar and be renowned throughout the whole earth."

12 ¹Then he ordered them to lead her into the room where his silver dinnerware was kept, and ordered them to set a table for her with his own delicacies to eat and his own wine to drink. ²But Judith said, "I cannot eat any of them, because it would be a scandal.

---

plans to go out of the camp into the valley every night to pray (11:17). When the critical moment comes, the two women will be able to leave the Assyrian camp with no challenge. Judith is indeed wise, as Holofernes says (11:20). He is so impressed by her holiness that he promises to abandon his god and worship Judith's God if he is successful in destroying Bethulia! It becomes ever clearer that he does not know what he is saying. He will destroy the Israelites and their sanctuary and then will worship their God? Poor Holofernes is totally befuddled!

JUDITH IN THE ASSYRIAN CAMP AND AT HOLOFERNES'S TENT

Judith 12

Judith sets up a pattern for her life in the Assyrian camp that will ensure her security when she carries out her plot. She has been given a certain amount of freedom. She has her own tent and keeps her own schedule. She continues to observe the dietary laws, refusing the delicacies that Holofernes orders for her. She also goes out every night with her maid to the valley of Bethulia to purify herself and pray for wisdom to succeed in her venture. She keeps to this rhythm for four days and waits. Holofernes is also waiting. He is concerned that she will run out of the food she can eat and he has no idea how he can get more for her. She reassures him that

Besides, I will have enough with the things I brought with me." ³Holofernes asked her, "But if your provisions give out, where can we get more of the same to provide for you? None of your people are with us." ⁴Judith answered him, "As surely as you live, my lord, your servant will not use up her supplies before the Lord accomplishes by my hand what he has determined."

⁵Then the attendants of Holofernes led her to her tent, where she slept until the middle of the night. Toward the early morning watch, she rose ⁶and sent this message to Holofernes, "Give orders, my lord, to let your servant go out for prayer." ⁷So Holofernes ordered his guards not to hinder her. Thus she stayed in the camp three days. Each night she went out to the valley of Bethulia, where she bathed herself at the spring of the camp. ⁸After bathing,

she prayed to the Lord, the God of Israel, to direct her way for the triumph of her people. ⁹Then she returned purified to the tent and remained there until her food was brought to her toward evening.

Judith at the Banquet of Holofernes. ¹⁰On the fourth day Holofernes gave a banquet for his servants alone, to which he did not invite any of the officers. ¹¹And he said to Bagoas, the eunuch in charge of his personal affairs, "Go and persuade the Hebrew woman in your care to come and to eat and drink with us. ¹²It would bring shame on us to be with such a woman without enjoying her. If we do not seduce her, she will laugh at us."

¹³So Bagoas left the presence of Holofernes, and came to Judith and said, "So lovely a maidservant should not be reluctant to come to my lord to

she will have enough to last until "the Lord accomplishes by [her] hand what he has determined" (12:4). Holofernes is completely blind to what her plan is.

Judith's insistence on eating the proper food described in Leviticus (see Lev 11) is not just part of her plot. It is a common practice in the postexilic period. During the Babylonian exile, the best way the Jews had to preserve their identity was through the ritual laws. They had no temple; they had no land. But they could still keep the laws of circumcision and proper diet. Tobit insists that during the Assyrian captivity he, unlike his fellow captives, never ate the Gentile food (Tob 1:10). Esther asserts that she has not eaten at the banquets of either the king or Haman (Esth 14:17[C:28]). During the persecution by the Syrian Antiochus IV Epiphanes, the Jews were willing even to suffer torture and martyrdom rather than eat forbidden food (1 Macc 1:62; 2 Macc 6:18-31; 7:1-2). Daniel convinces King Nebuchadnezzar of Babylon to give him and his companions only proper food (Dan 1:8-16).

By the fourth day Holofernes cannot stand it any longer. He sends his personal attendant, Bagoas, to persuade Judith to come and enjoy a meal

be honored by him, to enjoy drinking wine with us, and to act today like one of the Assyrian women who serve in the palace of Nebuchadnezzar." [14]Judith replied, "Who am I to refuse my lord? Whatever is pleasing to him I will promptly do. This will be a joy for me until the day of my death."

[15]So she proceeded to put on her festive garments and all her finery. Meanwhile her servant went ahead and spread out on the ground opposite Holofernes the fleece Bagoas had furnished for her daily use in reclining while eating. [16]Then Judith came in and reclined. The heart of Holofernes was in rapture over her and his passion was aroused. He was burning with the desire to possess her, for he had been biding his time to seduce her from the day he saw her. [17]Holofernes said to her, "Drink and be happy with us!" [18]Judith replied, "I will gladly drink, my lord, for today is the greatest day of my whole life." [19]She then took the things her servant had prepared and ate and drank in his presence. [20]Holofernes, charmed by her, drank a great quantity of wine, more than he had ever drunk on any day since he was born.

13 **Judith Beheads Holofernes.** [1]When it grew late, his servants quickly withdrew. Bagoas closed the tent from the outside and dismissed the attendants

---

with him. The irony continues. Holofernes calls Judith "the Hebrew woman." Does he not even know her name? He certainly does not know her intentions. He intends to seduce her, but she has already seduced him. Bagoas persuades her, the Hebrew woman, to come to Holofernes's tent and act like the Assyrian women. Her reply seems to indicate agreement, but the ambiguity again turns on the meaning of "her lord." She will never refuse her Lord and throughout her life will do "[w]hatever is pleasing to him" (12:14). She is delighted at the opportunity. She will declare to Holofernes that "today is the greatest day of [her] whole life" (12:18). Indeed it is. Her actions on this night will define her and bring her fame.

Again Judith beautifies herself and dresses up in "all her finery." One wonders how much luggage the women carried across the valley! Her maid goes ahead of her to Holofernes's tent to spread out fleece for her to recline to eat. The maid is going to have a much more significant role as the evening progresses, but Holofernes certainly does not even notice her. He is besotted by Judith's beauty and drinks far too much. His overindulgence will prove to be his undoing.

JUDITH BEHEADS HOLOFERNES AND RETURNS TO BETHULIA

Judith 13

The stage is set for the execution of Judith's plan. Holofernes is unconscious. His servants are also all asleep. Judith's maid is on the watch. The

from their master's presence. They went off to their beds, for they were all tired because the banquet had lasted so long. ²Judith was left alone in the tent with Holofernes, who lay sprawled on his bed, for he was drunk with wine. ³Judith had ordered her maidservant to stand outside the bedchamber and to wait, as on the other days, for her to come out; she had said she would be going out for her prayer. She had also said this same thing to Bagoas.

⁴When all had departed, and no one, small or great, was left in the bedchamber, Judith stood by Holofernes' bed and prayed silently, "O Lord, God of all might, in this hour look graciously on the work of my hands for the exaltation of Jerusalem. ⁵Now is the time for aiding your heritage and for carrying out my design to shatter the enemies who have risen against us." ⁶She went to the bedpost near the head of Holofernes, and taking his sword from it, ⁷she drew close to the bed, grasped the hair of his head, and said, "Strengthen me this day, Lord, God of Israel!" ⁸Then with all her might she struck his neck twice and cut off his head. ⁹She rolled his body off the bed

guards assume that both women will go out for prayer. Even Bagoas expects their regular predawn departure. Judith makes her final preparation by turning to God in prayer. She calls on the Lord as the "God of all might" (13:4). It is God's strength on which she depends. But she also mentions again her own hands, the hands of a woman. She reminds God that Jerusalem and this people belong to God in a special way as the divine heritage. Everything is now in readiness.

With one hand Judith takes hold of Holofernes's hair. After another prayer for strength, she takes hold of Holofernes's sword with the other hand and decapitates him. She may have been strengthened by God, but it is still a woman's hand that does the deed. It takes her two blows to cut off his head. But she is not a weak woman; she does not faint at the sight and smell of blood. With cool determination she rolls the body off the bed, takes the canopy as part of her proof, and goes out of the tent with Holofernes's head. The maid is not excitable either. Judith hands the head to the maid, who puts it in the food bag, and the two women go out toward the valley as usual for prayer. The whole action is completed calmly and quietly in a mere seven verses.

This portrayal of Judith reflects earlier biblical stories. When Deborah was judge over Israel, she predicted that Sisera, the general attacking them, would fall "into a woman's power" (Judg 4:9). And so it happened. Sisera fled to the tent of Jael, who lured him in with kind words, covered him with a rug, and then gave him milk to drink. Then this tent-dwelling woman hammered a tent peg through his head. When Barak, the general

The Return of Judith *by Botticelli, ca. 1470*

and took the canopy from its posts. Soon afterward, she came out and handed over the head of Holofernes to her maid, [10]who put it into her food bag. Then the two went out together for prayer as they were accustomed to do.

Judith and Her Maid Return to Bethulia. They passed through the camp, and skirting that valley, went up the mountain to Bethulia, and approached its gates. [11]From a distance, Judith shouted to the guards at the gates: "Open! Open the gate! God, our God, is with us. Once more he has shown his strength in Israel and his power against the enemy, as he has today!"

Judith Displays the Head of Holofernes. [12]When the citizens heard her voice, they hurried down to their city gate and sum-

moned the elders of the city. [13]All the people, from the least to the greatest, hurriedly assembled, for her return seemed unbelievable. They opened the gate and welcomed the two women. They made a fire for light and gathered around the two. [14]Judith urged them with a loud voice: "Praise God, give praise! Praise God, who has not withdrawn his mercy from the house of Israel, but has shattered our enemies by my hand this very night!" [15]Then she took the head out of the bag, showed it to them, and said: "Here is the head of Holofernes, the ranking general of the Assyrian forces, and here is the canopy under which he lay in his drunkenness. The Lord struck him down by the hand of a female! [16]Yet I swear by the Lord,

of the Israelite tribes, arrived, Jael presented him with the corpse (Judg 4:17-22). Later, when the people are threatened by their archenemy, the Philistines, David slays their champion, Goliath, with a slingshot and cuts off his head with Goliath's own sword (1 Sam 17:40-51). The figure of Judith is modeled on these earlier heroes.

Judith and her maid do not go into the valley, however. Rather they go around it and up the mountain to Bethulia. When they reach the gates, Judith cries out to the guards to open the gate and immediately gives credit to God for her success in defeating their enemy (13:10b-11). All the people gather around her and Judith strongly urges them again to give praise to God who has shattered the enemy. Judith will not claim the role of hero; she is simply God's helper in their rescue. She demonstrates her success by showing Holofernes's head and declares again that God has defeated him by the "hand of a female" (13:15). She also insists that she has not been dishonored by Holofernes, but has seduced him only by the beauty of her face.

The people follow her direction and begin to praise God. But Uzziah, who could only imagine their rescue in terms of rain, now praises Judith and declares her "blessed among women." Two other biblical women receive a similar praise, Jael in the Old Testament and Mary in the New Testament (Judg 5:24; Luke 1:42). All three women have been used by God to

who has protected me in the way I have walked, that it was my face that seduced Holofernes to his ruin, and that he did not defile me with sin or shame."

[17]All the people were greatly astonished. They bowed down and worshiped God, saying with one accord, "Blessed are you, our God, who today have humiliated the enemies of your people." [18]Then Uzziah said to her, "Blessed are you, daughter, by the Most High God, above all the women on earth; and blessed be the Lord God, the creator of heaven and earth, who guided your blow at the head of the leader of our enemies. [19]Your deed of hope will never be forgotten by those who recall the might of God. [20]May God make this redound to your everlasting honor, rewarding you with blessings, because you risked your life when our people were being oppressed, and you averted our disaster, walking in the straight path before our God."

And all the people answered, "Amen! Amen!"

V. Victory and Thanksgiving

14 **Judith's Plan of Attack.** [1]Then Judith said to them: "Listen to me, my brothers and sisters. Take this head and hang it on the parapet of your wall. [2]At daybreak, when the sun rises on the earth, each of you seize your weapons, and let all the able-bodied men rush out of the city under command of a captain, as if about to go down into the valley against the Assyrian patrol, but without going down. [3]The Assyrians will seize their weapons and hurry to their camp to awaken the generals of the army. When they run to the tent of Holofernes and do not find him, panic will seize them, and they will flee before you. [4]Then you and all the other inhabitants of the whole territory of Israel will pursue them and strike them down in their tracks. [5]But

defeat the enemy who threatened their people. Jael defeated Sisera; Judith defeated Holofernes. Mary, through her Son, has defeated Satan. All three women have performed a "deed of hope" that "will never be forgotten" (13:19). All the people who hear Uzziah's praise of Judith respond, "Amen! Amen!"

THE PEOPLE'S VICTORY OVER THE ENEMY

Judith 14

Judith's plan is not finished, even though the people of Bethulia are already celebrating. Holofernes is dead, but the Assyrian army is still encamped outside their walls. It is not yet daybreak and the Bethulians must act quickly. Judith has one more plan of deceit. She instructs the people to hang Holofernes's head on the parapet of the wall and then to rush out of the city armed for attack. But they are not to engage the Assyrians. They are simply to wait and let the enemy see them. When the Assyrians

before doing this, summon for me Achior the Ammonite, that he may see and recognize the one who despised the house of Israel and sent him here to meet his death."

Achior's Conversion. ⁶So they called Achior from the house of Uzziah. When he came and saw the head of Holofernes in the hand of one of the men in the assembly of the people, he collapsed in a faint. ⁷Then, after they lifted him up, he threw himself at the feet of Judith in homage, saying: "Blessed are you in every tent of Judah! In every nation, all who hear your name will be struck with terror. ⁸But now, tell me all that you did during these days." So Judith told him, in the midst of the people, all that she had done, from the day she left until the time she began speaking to them. ⁹When she had finished her account, the people cheered loudly, so that the city resounded with shouts of joy. ¹⁰Now Achior, seeing all that the God of Israel had done, believed firmly in God. He circumcised the flesh of his foreskin and he has been united with the house of Israel to the present day.

Panic in the Assyrian Camp. ¹¹At daybreak they hung the head of Holofernes on the wall. Then all the Israelite men took up their weapons and went out by groups to the mountain passes. ¹²When the Assyrians saw them, they notified their commanders, who, in turn, went to their generals, their division leaders, and all their other leaders. ¹³They came to the tent of Holofernes and said to the one in charge of all his things, "Awaken our lord, for the slaves have dared come down against us in battle, to their utter destruction." ¹⁴So Bagoas went in and knocked at the entry of the tent,

---

muster for battle, they will discover that they are without a leader and will flee demoralized.

One more task remains, however, before this plan can be carried out. Achior, who has met Holofernes, must be summoned to verify that the severed head is indeed that of the Assyrian leader. In contrast to Judith and her maid, who were cool and collected at the crucial moment, Achior faints at the sight of Holofernes's head. When he is revived, he too praises Judith and calls her blessed. He also wisely realizes that every enemy of Israel will be terrified to hear her name. Then he asks Judith to retell the story, which gives the people another chance to cheer for joy. Achior is so moved by her courage and the power of God that he asks for circumcision and embraces the faith of Judith's people.

The people obey Judith's instructions, and, as planned, the Assyrians prepare for battle. They assume that they will slaughter the Israelites because of their superior numbers and weapons. But they have not yet realized the effects of Judith's trickery. Bagoas presumes she is still in Holofernes's tent, but he is shocked to find his master dead on the floor. He is even more dismayed to realize that Holofernes's head is missing, a

presuming that Holofernes was sleeping with Judith. ¹⁵When no one answered, he parted the curtains, entered the bedchamber, and found him thrown on the floor dead, with his head gone! ¹⁶He cried out loudly, weeping, groaning, and howling, and tore his garments. ¹⁷Then he entered the tent where Judith had her quarters; and, not finding her, he rushed out to the troops and cried: ¹⁸"The slaves have duped us! One Hebrew woman has brought shame on the house of King Nebuchadnezzar. Look! Holofernes on the ground— without a head!"

¹⁹When the leaders of the Assyrian forces heard these words, they tore their tunics and were overcome with great distress. Their loud cries and shouts were heard throughout the camp.

15 ¹On hearing what had happened, those still in their tents were horrified. ²Overcome with fear and dread, no one kept ranks any longer. They scattered in all directions, and fled along every path, both through the valley and in the hill country. ³Those who were stationed in the hill country around Bethulia also took to flight. Then

---

fact that is repeated twice. The startling news does indeed demoralize the Assyrian troops and they flee in terror.

CELEBRATION OF VICTORY; PRAISE OF JUDITH

Judith 15

As the Assyrian troops flee, the Israelite soldiers attack them. But now they are not alone. All the Israelites from Galilee in the north to Jerusalem in the south and Gilead to the east come to join the battle. They drive the Assyrians even as far north as Damascus. All this military force has apparently been waiting to see the fate of Bethulia before they took action.

The report of plundering the Assyrians is equally exaggerated. The people of Bethulia first plunder the camp, then all the soldiers who returned from the slaughter. Towns and villages all around take their share. They spend thirty days gathering up the plunder. It seems the whole country is enriched with the goods in the Assyrian camp. Judith too gets her share of the goods, everything of value that was in Holofernes's tent. Ever resourceful, she hitches up her mule cart and takes the bounty home. She is now even more wealthy than before. The description is amazing. Why was all this wealth in the camp of a besieging army? Did they leave nothing behind for Nebuchadnezzar? The point seems to be that the Assyrians are totally defeated and the Israelites now totally secure.

The celebration is not only about riches, however. The officials from Jerusalem come to see what has happened and to congratulate Judith. They sing another blessing over her and all the people respond with their

the Israelites, every warrior among them, came charging down upon them.

⁴Uzziah sent messengers to Betomasthaim, to Choba and Kona, and to the whole territory of Israel to report what had happened and to urge them all to attack the enemy and destroy them. ⁵On hearing this, all the Israelites, with one accord, attacked them and cut them down as far as Choba. Even those from Jerusalem and the rest of the hill country took part in this, for they too had been notified of the happenings in the camp of their enemy. The Gileadites and the Galileans struck the enemy's flanks with great slaughter, even beyond Damascus and its borders. ⁶The remaining people of Bethulia swept down on the camp of the Assyrians, plundered it, and acquired great riches. ⁷The Israelites, when they returned from the slaughter, took possession of what was left. Even the towns and villages in the hill country and on the plain got an enormous quantity of spoils, for there was a tremendous amount of it.

Israel Celebrates Judith's Victory.
⁸Then the high priest Joakim and the senate of the Israelites who lived in Je-

rusalem came to see for themselves the good things that the Lord had done for Israel, and to meet and congratulate Judith. ⁹When they came to her, all with one accord blessed her, saying:

"You are the glory of Jerusalem!
You are the great pride of Israel!
You are the great boast of our nation!
¹⁰By your own hand you have done all this.
You have done good things for Israel,
and God is pleased with them.
May the Almighty Lord bless you forever!"
And all the people said, "Amen!"

¹¹For thirty days all the people plundered the camp, giving Judith the tent of Holofernes, with all his silver, his beds, his dishes, and all his furniture. She took them and loaded her mule, hitched her carts, and loaded these things on them.

¹²All the women of Israel gathered to see her, and they blessed her and performed a dance in her honor. She took branches in her hands and distributed them to the women around her, ¹³and she and the other women crowned themselves with olive leaves. Then, at

---

Amen. These leaders also note that the victory was won by the hand of Judith. Their blessing is now sung for feasts of the Blessed Virgin Mary, another woman who contributed to the salvation of her people.

Finally, in the tradition of holy war, the women perform the victory dance. The tradition begins with Miriam, who leads all the women in celebrating God's deliverance of the people at the Reed Sea (Exod 15). A more tragic example is that of Jephthah's daughter, who, not knowing that her father had promised to give thanks by sacrificing the first living thing that came out of his house, rushes out with song and dance to celebrate his victory over the Ammonites (Judg 11:34). There is no thought of tragedy in Judith's victory dance, however. All the women crown themselves with

the head of all the people, she led the women in the dance, while the men of Israel followed, bearing their weapons, wearing garlands and singing songs of praise. [14]Judith led all Israel in this song of thanksgiving, and the people loudly sang this hymn of praise:

Judith's Hymn of Deliverance

16 [1]And Judith sang:

"Strike up a song to my God with
  tambourines,
  sing to the Lord with cymbals;
Improvise for him a new song,
  exalt and acclaim his name.
[2]For the Lord is a God who crushes
  wars;
  he sets his encampment among
  his people;
  he delivered me from the hands
  of my pursuers.

[3]"The Assyrian came from the
  mountains of the north,
  with myriads of his forces he
  came;
Their numbers blocked the wadis,
  their cavalry covered the hills.
[4]He threatened to burn my territory,
  put my youths to the sword,
Dash my infants to the ground,
  seize my children as plunder.
And carry off my virgins as
  spoil.

[5]"But the Lord Almighty thwarted
  them,
  by the hand of a female!
[6]Not by youths was their champion
  struck down,
  nor did Titans bring him low,
  nor did tall giants attack him;
But Judith, the daughter of Merari,
  by the beauty of her face
  brought him down.

olive leaves, while even the men join in the singing. The words of Judith's song follow in the next chapter.

JUDITH'S THANKSGIVING SONG

Judith 16:1-17

Judith's song is modeled on the songs of thanksgiving in the book of Psalms. This form is more fluid than the lament or the hymn, but there are some standard elements that appear frequently. Often the grateful person turns first to God with thanksgiving and then gathers a crowd and tells the story of rescue. Gathering a crowd is described at the end of chapter 15. Judith's song then begins like a hymn, with a call to everyone to sing praise (16:1; cf. Ps 33:3; 96:1; 98:1; 147:7; 149:1; 150:5) and an announcement of the reasons for praise (16:2; cf. Ps 46:9-10). The reasons for praise, which lead into the formal thanksgiving, echo David's song of thanksgiving when he had been rescued from Saul (2 Sam 22:4; Ps 18:4).

The story of rescue begins in verse 3. In order to show how great God's deliverance was, the distress is described in exaggerated terms, balancing the description of Holofernes's force in the opening chapters (16:3-4; cf.

⁷She took off her widow's garb
  to raise up the afflicted in Israel.
She anointed her face with fragrant
    oil;
  ⁸fixed her hair with a diadem,
  and put on a linen robe to
      beguile him.
⁹Her sandals ravished his eyes,
  her beauty captivated his mind,
  the sword cut through his neck!

¹⁰"The Persians trembled at her
    boldness,
  the Medes were daunted at her
    daring.
¹¹When my lowly ones shouted,
  and my weak ones cried out,
The enemy was terrified,
  screamed and took to flight.
¹²Sons of maidservants pierced
    them through;
  wounded them like deserters'
    children.

They perished before the ranks
  of my Lord.

¹³"I will sing a new song to my God.
  O Lord, great are you and
    glorious,
  marvelous in power and unsur-
    passable.
¹⁴Let your every creature serve you;
  for you spoke, and they were
    made.
You sent forth your spirit, and it
    created them;
  no one can resist your voice.
¹⁵For the mountains to their bases
  are tossed with the waters;
  the rocks, like wax, melt before
    your glance.

"But to those who fear you,
  you will show mercy.
¹⁶Though the sweet fragrance of
  every sacrifice is a trifle,

2:4-18; 7:1-3). The rescue is equally dramatic (16:5-12). First of all, Judith describes herself and how God worked through her. The enemy is destroyed "by the hand of a female," a great humiliation. The point is driven home by naming possible foes of great strength, Titans and giants. However, it was not power that overcame Holofernes, but the beauty of a woman. Judith has prepared for battle by beautifying herself, and God has worked through that beauty. After the lavish description of her loveliness, the brutality of the final line is a shock: "the sword cut through his neck!" (16:9).

The Persians and Medes are a surprise (16:10). Nebuchadnezzar has been introduced as the king of the Assyrians, and Holofernes is the general of the Assyrian army (1:1, 7, 11; 2:1, 4; 4:1). It is the Assyrian army that has besieged Bethulia (7:17; 8:9; 9:7) and that has now fled before the people of Bethulia (14:3, 19; 15:1-6). Historically, Nebuchadnezzar was king of the Babylonians, who destroyed Jerusalem in 587 B.C. and took its people into exile. The Babylonian empire was later defeated by a coalition of Persians and Medes under Cyrus, king of Persia. It is Cyrus who in 538 B.C. allowed the Jews to return home from the Babylonian exile. The author of this story of Judith is again gathering every possible threat against Judah and Israel to show how great God's rescue was. As the

and the fat of all burnt offerings
but little in your sight,
one who fears the Lord is forever great.

¹⁷"Woe to the nations that rise
against my people!

the Lord Almighty will requite
them;
in the day of judgment he will
punish them:
He will send fire and worms into
their flesh,

wisdom literature continually asserts, God works through the lowly and the humble to defeat the strong (16:11-12; cf. Sir 10:14-15).

Judith now returns to a song of praise, speaking again to God, who is great and glorious and powerful (16:13-15; cf. Ps 21:6; 66:2; 118:14). God is the one who created everything by the word, filling creatures with the divine spirit (see Gen 1:3, 6, 9, 11, 14, 20, 24, 26; Gen 2:7; Ps 33:9; 104:30; 148:5). God's word is so powerful that even the "mountains melt like wax" (Ps 97:5; cf. Mic 1:3-4). Those who fear the Lord, however, will be exalted and treated with mercy (cf. Ps 31:20; 33:18; 34:8, 10; 40:4; 103:13; 115:11). Fear of the Lord is awe at God's greatness and God's compassion. It is a spirit of wonder at all God's goodness and a dread of ever offending God. Fear of the Lord is the way to everything good (Sir 1:11-30). The song of thanksgiving often concludes with a pilgrimage to the sanctuary to offer sacrifice to God. In Judith's hymn the fear of the Lord is described as even better than sacrifice (16:16). But the ritual offering will be performed as soon as the song is over (16:18).

Judith's song ends with a woe (16:17). In this final verse there is a suggestion of belief in life after death. There will be punishment for the enemies of God's people on the "day of judgment." The punishment will include "fire and worms," a description of hell. Their suffering will last "forever." This signals a transition from the idea that all human beings, good and bad, went to Sheol when they died, to a belief that the good went to heaven and the bad to hell. Sheol was not a place of punishment; rather it was more like our earlier concept of limbo. But once the belief in everlasting life developed, Sheol was transformed into hell. This transition is illustrated in the book of Sirach. The Hebrew version, from the original author, says, "More and more, humble your pride; / what awaits mortals is worms" (Sir 7:17). The grandson's translation into Greek, however, says, "Humble yourself to the utmost, / for the punishment of the ungodly is fire and worms" (Sir 7:17, NRSV). The grandfather thought everyone went to Sheol; the grandson believed that only the "ungodly" went there, and that it was now a place of suffering and fire. The author of Judith's song agrees with the grandson.

and they will weep and suffer forever."

¹⁸When they arrived at Jerusalem, they worshiped God. As soon as the people were purified, they offered their burnt offerings, voluntary offerings, and donations. ¹⁹Judith dedicated to God all the things of Holofernes that the people had given her, putting under the ban the canopy that she herself had taken from his bedchamber. ²⁰For three months the people continued their celebration in Jerusalem before the sanctuary, and Judith remained with them.

The Renown and Death of Judith. ²¹When those days were over, all of them returned to their inheritance. Judith went back to Bethulia and remained on her estate. For the rest of her life she was renowned throughout the land. ²²Many wished to marry her, but she gave herself to no man all the days of

HAPPILY EVER AFTER

Judith 16:18-25

After the song, the people go to Jerusalem to worship God. Those who had touched the dead body of Holofernes must spend seven days being purified according to the Torah legislation (Num 19:11-13). Then they offer three types of sacrifice: burnt offerings, which are wholly offered to God (Lev 1; 6:1-6); voluntary offerings, which must be eaten within two days (Lev 7:16); and various donations. Deuteronomy remarks that, in the context of the feast of Weeks, voluntary offerings should be "in proportion to the blessing" the Lord has granted (Deut 16:10). The people of Bethulia must be making very generous offerings, since their blessing is nothing short of rescue from certain death. Their joy is evident in the length of time of the celebration: three months!

Judith also donates all Holofernes's things and puts his canopy under the ban. This "ban" is part of the restrictions of holy war in Israel's early history. The people are not to profit from making war; whatever spoils they take are "doomed" (Hebrew *herem*) or put under the ban. In the pioneer period, if the defeated people were not residents of the Promised Land, a share of the spoils was donated to the sanctuary for sacrifice or for the support of the priests and Levites, and the rest could be shared among the people (see Num 18:14; 31:9-12, 25-47; but compare Deut 20:10-15).

When the celebration is over, Judith returns to her estate and lives in relative seclusion. Before she died she made arrangements to distribute her wealth to her own family and to her in-laws. She also set her maid free, but it is not clear when this happens. Is it immediately? Is it an instruction to be followed at the end of her life? Perhaps the maid continued to live with her until she died at the ripe old age of 105. Throughout her

her life from the time her husband, Manasseh, died and was gathered to his people. ²³Her fame continued to increase, and she lived in the house of her husband, reaching the advanced age of one hundred and five. She set her maid free. And when she died in Bethulia, they buried her in the cave of her husband, Manasseh; ²⁴and the house of Israel mourned her for seven days. Before she died, she distributed her property to the relatives of her husband, Manasseh, and to her own relatives.

²⁵During the lifetime of Judith and for a long time after her death, no one ever again spread terror among the Israelites.

---

life she, like the judges before her, was a protection for the Israelites (cf. Judg 3:11, 30; 5:31; 8:28). At her death the people mourned her for the customary period of seven days (cf. Sir 22:12a).

REVIEW AIDS AND DISCUSSION TOPICS

The Book of Jonah *(pages 7–17)*

1. What do we know about the identities of Amittai's son Jonah and the prophet Jonah?

2. The book of Jonah can be viewed as a parable, satire, or parody. Discuss how the story can fit into each of these interpretations.

3. Although the book of Jonah is considered to be fictional, how is it an important part of the theme of the Book of the Twelve?

4. Describe how God is portrayed in this book. What is the overall message?

5. What literary devices are used in the book of Jonah? What is the significance of repeating the variant phrases of "go down"/"get up"?

6. Identify the pattern of the prayer Jonah says while in the belly of the fish (2:3-10).

7. Discuss the possibility of the fish being feminine and what that could mean.

8. How does the call of God to Jonah in the third chapter contrast with the call in the first chapter?

9. How is Jonah "defeated by his own success," and why is he angry (ch. 4)?

10. What is significant about the *qiqayon* plant in chapter 4?

The Book of Tobit *(pages 18–56)*

1. Despite Tobit's good character, what is his greatest flaw?

2. Why does the angel Raphael hide his identity until the end of the story?

3. Although the book of Tobit is a work of fiction, what can readers learn from this story?

4. Describe the historical background of this book.

5. How is Tobit's grandmother Deborah (1:8) an important influence on him?

6. Examine the role of Tobit's wife Anna in the story.

7. Discuss both the similarities and the differences between Tobit's prayer and Sarah's prayer (3:2-6, 11-15).

8. Compare chapter 4 to farewell discourses in Genesis 47:29–49:33; Joshua 22–24; and 1 Chronicles 28–29.

9. What is ironic about this story, starting in chapter 5?

10. In Tobit 6:3, a large fish tries to swallow Tobiah's foot. What does this fish come to symbolize?

11. Why does Raguel state in 7:11 that Tobiah and Sarah are brother and sister?

12. Compare Tobit 8:6 to Genesis 2:18. How is the mention of Adam and Eve different in the book of Tobit compared to other Bible books (besides Genesis)?

13. Tobit and Anna have very different reactions to Tobiah's delay (ch. 10). With which of them do you relate?

14. How can Anna's reaction to Tobiah's homecoming be interpreted (11:6, 9)?

15. What is Raphael's purpose in this story (ch. 12)?

16. Compare Raphael to the angels Michael (Dan 10:13, 21; 12:1; Rev 12:7-9) and Gabriel (Dan 8:16; 9:21; Luke 1:11-19, 26-38), and discuss the topic of angelology.

17. Summarize the points Tobit makes in his song of praise in chapter 13.

18. Why does Tobit tell Tobiah and his sons the story of Ahiqar and Nadin (14:10)?

The Book of Judith *(pages 57–99)*

1. What is paradoxical about Judith's character?

2. There is an important purpose of this fictional story—what is it?

3. Consider the question of "Who is God?" throughout the book of Judith.

4. What can readers conclude about the historical inaccuracies and exaggeration of this book (ch. 1)?

5. Discuss the portrayal of Nebuchadnezzar as a god in chapter 2.

6. How does Judith 4:13 compare to Tobit 3:16-17?

7. What Deuteronomic principle does Achior allude to in 5:17-18, 20-21?

8. The importance of Achior's role becomes evident in chapter 6—how so?

9. What is the significance of the number thirty-four in chapter 7?

10. The character of Judith is finally introduced in chapter 8. How is she described in verses 1-8?

11. What is Uzziah's reaction to the advice Judith gives to the elders (8:11-27)?

12. Why does Judith refer to the story of Simeon in her prayer (ch. 9)?

13. What are Judith's "weapons" in chapters 10–12?

14. How does Judith deceive Holofernes in chapter 11?

15. Why does Judith have certain dietary requirements while staying in Holofernes's camp (ch. 12)?

16. Compare Judith (ch. 13) to Jael (Judg 4:17-22) and to David (1 Sam 17:40-51).

17. What does Judith have in common with both Jael and Mary (Judg 5:24; Luke 1:42)?

18. Reflect on Judith 15:9-10 as a passage in praise of the Blessed Virgin Mary.

19. What do the statements in Judith 16:17 indicate about beliefs in the afterlife?

INDEX OF CITATIONS FROM THE
CATECHISM OF THE CATHOLIC CHURCH

The arabic number(s) following the citation refer to the paragraph number(s) in the *Catechism of the Catholic Church*. The asterisk following a paragraph number indicates that the citation has been paraphrased.

Jonah		2:12-18 Vulg.	312*	12:8	1434*
1:3	29*	3:11-16	2585*	12:12	336*
2:1	627*	4:3-4	2214*	13:2	269*
2:3-10	2585*	4:5-11	2447*		
		4:15	1789*		
Tobit		8:4-9	2361	**Judith**	
1:16-18	2300*	8:6	360*	9:2-14	2585*

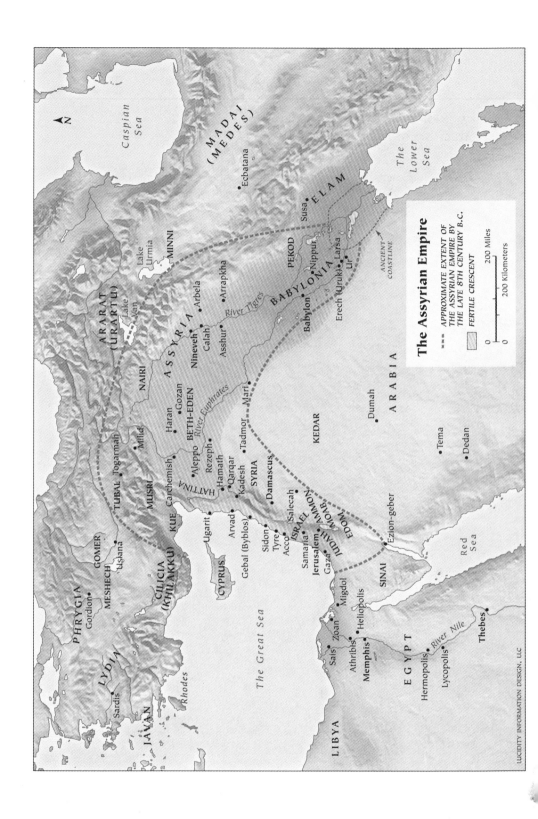

The Assyrian Empire

APPROXIMATE EXTENT OF
THE ASSYRIAN EMPIRE BY
THE LATE 8TH CENTURY B.C.

FERTILE CRESCENT

0   200 Miles

0   200 Kilometers

Caspian Sea

MADAI
(MEDES)

The Lower Sea

• Ecbatana

MINNI

ELAM

• Susa

PEKOD

Lake Urmia

ASSYRIA

BABYLONIA

Nippur •
Larsa •

ANCIENT COASTLINE

ARARAT
(URARTU)

Lake Van

• Arbela

• Arrapkha

Ur •

Erech (Uruk) •

River Tigris

• Nineveh
• Calah
• Asshur

Babylon •

NAIRI

Haran •
Gozan •

BETH-EDEN

• Tadmor   Mari •

ARABIA

MUSRI

Milid •

Togarmah •

Aleppo •
Rezeph •

Hamath •

River Euphrates

Dumah •

KEDAR

TUBAL

Carchemish •

KUE

Qarqar •
Kadesh •

HATTINA

SYRIA

• Damascus

• Tema

• Dedan

PHRYGIA

GOMER

Ushana •

CILICIA
(KHILAKKU)

Ugarit •

Arvad •

Saleech •

AMMON

MOAB

EDOM

Gordion •

MESHECH

Sidon •
Tyre •
Acco •

Gebal (Byblos) •

Samaria •

ISRAEL

JUDAH

Ezion-geber •

Red Sea

LYDIA

CYPRUS

Jerusalem •

Gaza •

SINAI

Sardis •

Rhodes

Migdol •

Zoan •

Heliopolis •

JAVAN

The Great Sea

Sais •

Athribis •

Memphis •

Hermopolis •

EGYPT

River Nile

Lycopolis •

• Thebes

LIBYA

LUCIDITY INFORMATION DESIGN, LLC